Puccini's

LA BOHÈME

OPERA CLASSICS LIBRARY™

Edited by Burton D. Fisher
Principal lecturer, *Opera Journeys Lecture Series*

Opera Journeys™ Publishing / Coral Gables, Florida

OPERA CLASSICS LIBRARY ™

• Aida • The Barber of Seville • La Bohème • Carmen
• Cavalleria Rusticana • Così fan tutte • Don Giovanni
• Don Pasquale • The Elixir of Love • Elektra
• Eugene Onegin • Exploring Wagner's Ring • Falstaff
• Faust • The Flying Dutchman • Hansel and Gretel
• L'Italiana in Algeri • Julius Caesar • Lohengrin
• Lucia di Lammermoor • Macbeth • Madama Butterfly
• The Magic Flute • Manon • Manon Lescaut
• The Marriage of Figaro • A Masked Ball • The Mikado
• Otello • I Pagliacci • Porgy and Bess • The Rhinegold
• Rigoletto • Der Rosenkavalier • Salome • Samson and Delilah
• Siegfried • The Tales of Hoffmann • Tannhäuser
• Tosca • La Traviata • Il Trovatore • Turandot
• Twilight of the Gods • The Valkyrie

WEB SITE: operajourneys.com   E MAIL: operaj@bellsouth.net

"While the basis of Verdi's operas is a battle cry, the basis of Puccini's operas is a mating call."
-The critic Harold Schoenberg in comparing Verdi with Puccini

"I put all my soul into Bohème, and I love it boundlessly. I love its creatures more than I can say…."
-Giacomo Puccini

Contents

Prelude
OPERA CLASSICS LIBRARY's *LA BOHÈME*

LA BOHÈME, since its premiere in 1896, has remained one of the most popular and most performed operas worldwide. *OPERA CLASSICS LIBRARY* explores this wonder of the operatic world, its magic, its mystique, and its story's unusual relevancy to contemporary times.

The *Commentary and Analysis* offers pertinent biographical information about Puccini, his mind-set at the time of *LA BOHÈME's* composition, the genesis of the opera, its premiere and performance history, and insightful story and character analysis.

The text also contains a *Brief Story Synopsis, Principal Characters in La Bohème,* and a *Story Narrative with Music Highlight Examples,* the latter containing original music transcriptions that are interspersed appropriately within the story's dramatic exposition. In addition, the text includes a *Discography, Videography,* and a *Dictionary of Opera and Musical Terms.*

The *Libretto* has been newly translated by the Opera Journeys staff with specific emphasis on retaining a literal translation, but also with the objective to provide a faithful translation in modern and contemporary English; in this way, the substance of the drama becomes more intelligible. To enhance educational objectives, the *Libretto* also contains musical highlight examples interspersed within the drama.

The opera art form is the sum of many artistic expressions: theatrical drama, music, scenery, poetry, dance, acting and gesture. In opera, it is the composer who is the dramatist, using the emotive power of his music to express intense, human conflicts. Words evoke thoughts, but music provokes feelings; opera's sublime fusion of words, music and all the theatrical arts provides powerful theater, an impact on one's sensibilities that can reach into the very depths of the human soul. Puccini's *LA BOHÈME,* certainly a crown jewel of his glorious operatic inventions, remains a perennial sentimental favorite in the operatic canon, a tribute to the art form as well as to its ingenious composer.

Burton D. Fisher
Editor
OPERA CLASSICS LIBRARY

LA BOHÈME

Italian opera in four acts

Music
by
Giacomo Puccini

**Libretto by Giuseppe Giacosa and Luigi Illica,
adapted from the novel by Henri Murger,
Scènes de la vie de Bohème ("Scenes from Bohemian Life")**

**Premiere: Teatro Reggio, Turin, Italy,
February 1896.**

Commentary and Analysis

Giacomo Puccini — 1858 to 1924 — was the heir to Italy's cherished opera icon, Giuseppe Verdi: he became the last superstar of the great Italian opera tradition in which lyricism, melody and the vocal arts, dominated the art form.

Puccini came from a family of musicians who for generations had been church organists and composers in his native Lucca, Italy, a part of the Tuscany region. His operatic epiphany occurred when he heard a performance of Verdi's *Aida*: at that moment the eighteen year old budding composer became inspired toward a future in opera. With aid from Queen Margherita of Italy that was supplemented by additional funds from a great uncle, he progressed to the Milan Conservatory where he eventually studied under Amilcare Ponchielli, a renowned musician, teacher, and the composer of *La Gioconda* (1876).

In Milan, Ponchielli became his mentor and astutely recognized his extraordinarily rich orchestral and symphonic imagination, and his remarkable harmonic, and melodic inventiveness, resources that would become the hallmarks and prime characteristics of Puccini's mature compositional style.

Puccini's early experiences served to elevate his acute sense of drama, which eventually became engraved in his operatic works. He was fortunate to have been exposed to a wide range of dramatic plays that were presented in his hometown by distinguished touring companies: works by Vittorio Alfieri, Carlo Goldoni, the French works of Alexandre Dumas', father and son, as well as those of the extremely popular Victorien Sardou.

In 1884, at the age of 26, Puccini competed in the publisher Sonzogno's one-act opera contest with his lyric stage work, *Le Villi* ("The Witches"), a phantasmagoric romantic tale about abandoned young women who die of lovesickness. Musically and dramatically, *Le Villi* remains quite a distance from the poignant sentimentalism which later became Puccini's trademark. *Le Villi* lost the contest, but La Scala agreed to produce it for its following season. But more significantly to Puccini's future career, Giulio Ricordi, the influential publisher, recognized the young composer's talent to write music drama, and lured him from his competitor, Sonzogno.

Puccini became Ricordi's favorite composer, a status that developed into much peer envy, resentfulness, and jealousy among his rivals, as well as from Ricordi's chief publishing competitor, Sonzogno. Nevertheless, Ricordi used his ingenious golden touch to unite composers and librettists, and he proceeded to assemble the best poets and dramatists for his budding star, Puccini.

Ricordi commissioned Puccini to write a second opera, *Edgar* (1889), a melodrama involving a rivalry between two brothers for a seductive Moorish girl that erupts into powerful passions of betrayal and revenge. Its premiere at La Scala became a disappointment, the critics praising Puccini's orchestral and harmonic advancement from *Le Villi,* but considering the opera mediocre: even its later condensation from four to three acts could not redeem it or improve its fortunes.

Ricordi's faith in his young protege was triumphantly vindicated by the immediate success of Puccini's next opera, *Manon Lescaut* (1893). The genesis of the libretto was itself an operatic melodrama, saturated with feuds and disagreements between its considerable group of librettists who included Ruggiero Leoncavallo, Luigi Illica, Giuseppe Giacosa, Domenico Oliva, Marco Praga, and even Giulio Ricordi himself. The critics and public were unanimous in their praise of Puccini's third opera, and in London, the eminent critic, George Bernard Shaw, noted that in *Manon Lescaut,* "Puccini looks to me more like the heir of Verdi than any of his rivals."

For Puccini's librettos over the next decade, Ricordi secured for him the illustrious team of the scenarist, Luigi Illica, and the poet, playwright, and versifier, Giuseppe Giacosa. The first fruit of their collaboration became *La Bohème* (1896), drawn from Henry Murger's picaresque novel about life among the artists of the Latin Quarter in Paris during the 1830s: *Scènes de la vie de Bohème.*

The critics were strangely cool at *La Bohème*'s premiere, several of them finding it a restrained work when compared to the inventive passion and ardor of *Manon Lescaut.* But in spite of negative reviews, the public eventually became enamored with the opera, and it would only be in Vienna, where Mahler, hostile to Puccini, virtually banned *La Bohème* in favor of Leoncavallo's treatment of the same subject.

After *La Bohème,* Puccini went on to transform Victorien Sardou's play, *La Tosca,* into a sensational, powerful, and thrilling musical action drama, improving on his literary source and providing immortality to its dramatist.

His next opera adapted David Belasco's one-act play, *Madame Butterfly* (1904). At its premiere, the opera experienced what Puccini described as "a veritable lynching"; the audience's hostility and denunciation of the composer and his work were apparently deliberately engineered by rivals who were jealous of Puccini's success and favored status with Ricordi. Nevertheless, *Madama Butterfly* quickly joined its two predecessors as cornerstones of the contemporary operatic repertory.

Puccini followed with *La Fanciulla del West,* 1910 ("The Girl of the Golden West"), *La Rondine* (1917), the three one-act operas of *Il Trittico – Suor Angelica, Gianni Schicchi,* and *Il Tabarro* (1918), and his final work, *Turandot* (1925), completed posthumously by Franco Alfano under the direction of Arturo Toscanini.

Puccini's musical and dramatic style reflects the naturalistic movement of the "giovane scuola," the late nineteenth century Italian artistic genre called *verismo,* or Realism: these works emphasized swift dramatic action, and were thematically concentrated on raw human nature: the portrayal of problems and conflicts of characters in everyday situations. Throughout his career, Puccini identified himself with *verismo,* what he called the "stile mascagnano," the Mascagni style first successfully portrayed in *Cavalleria Rusticana* (1890).

In the Realism genre — *verismo* — no subject was too mundane, no subject was too harsh, and no subject was too ugly; therefore, the plots dealt with hot and heavy passions: sex, seduction, revenge, betrayal, jealousy, murder and death. In *verismo,* primal passions are the subject of the action: it portrays the latent animal, the uncivilized savage, and the barbarian part of man's soul; a confirmation of Darwin's theory that man evolved from primal beast. In Realism and its successors, modernity and *film noire,* man is portrayed as irrational, brutal, crude, cruel, and demonic.

In Realism, death became the consummation of desire: in Realism, good does not necessarily triumph over evil. In the Realism genre, Enlightenment's reason and

Romanticism's freedom and sentimentality were overturned: man became viewed as a creature of instinct.

Puccini wrote tonal music within the diatonic (whole tone) scale, but within that framework, his style has a strongly personal lyrical signature that is readily identifiable: lush melodies, occasional unresolved dissonances, and daring harmonic and instrumental colors; his writing endows both his vocal and orchestral works with a soft suppleness, elegance, gentleness as well as a poignancy.

In all of Puccini's works, leitmotifs — melodies identifying persons and ideas — play a prominent role and provide cohesion, emotion, and reminiscence, however, they are never developed to the systematic symphonic grandeur of Wagner, but are always wed and exploited for ultimate dramatic and symphonic effect.

Puccini's dramatic instincts never failed him; he was truly a master stage-craftsman with a consummate knowledge of the demands of the stage, and a pronounced feeling for theatrical effects, even, it can be argued, more concerned than Wagner to integrate his music, words, and gestures into a single conceptual unity. A perfect example of Puccini's stage genius occurs in the action ensemble of *Manon Lescaut*'s roll-call of the prostitutes, and *Tosca*'s "Te Deum."

Just like Bellini in his *I Puritani,* the music associated with Puccini's heroines — their leitmotif — is heard before the heroines themselves are seen: a brilliant dramatic technique evidenced in the entrances of Tosca, Butterfly, Manon Lescaut, and Mimi.

Puccini had a rare gift for evoking ambience: the bells in Act III of *Tosca* or the ship's sirens in *Il Tabarro*. In *La Bohème,* musical ambience or musical impressions convey realistic and minute details of everyday life: Rodolfo's manuscript being burned in the fire; the sound effects from Colline tumbling down the hall; Schaunard's horn; and the falling snowflakes at the start of Act III. Debussy, no friend to the contemporary school of Italian opera, was prompted to confess to Paul Dukas that he knew of no one who had described the Paris of the age of Louis-Philippe "as well as Puccini in *La Bohème.*"

Puccini, with the exception of his last opera, *Turandot,* was not a composer of ambitious works or grand opera: works presenting stage spectacle in the manner of Meyerbeer, Verdi or Wagner. He commented that "the only music I can make is of small things," acknowledging that his talent and temperament were not suited to works of large design, spectacle, or portrayals of romantic heroism.

Indeed, *La Bohème* does not deal with the world of kings, nobles, gods, or heroes, but rather, in its realism, it portrays simple, ordinary people, and the countless little humdrum details of their everyday lives. Certainly, *La Bohème* epitomizes Puccini's world of "small things," its grandeur not of supercharged passions evolving from world-shattering events, but rather from moments of tender, poignant lyrical emotion and pathos.

Ultimately, in the writing of dramas filled with tenderness and beauty, Puccini had no equals, and few equals in inventing a personal lyricism that portrayed intimate humanity with sentimentalism and beauty. Specifically in *La Bohème,* Puccini creates a perfect balance between realism and romanticism, as well as between comedy and pathos.

Puccini's writing for both voice and orchestra is rich and elegant. His supreme talent was his magic for inventive melody which he expressed in a combination of outstanding instrumental coloration and harmonic texture: a signature that is so individual that it is recognized immediately. Puccini's memorable arias are endlessly haunting: one leaves a Puccini opera performance, but the music never leaves the listener.

La Bohème is based on Henri Murger's *Scènes de la vie de Bohème* ("Scenes from Bohemian Life"), a series of picaresque autobiographical sketches and episodes drawn from Murger's own experiences as a struggling writer in Paris in the 1830s: the story first appeared serialized for a magazine, and later with huge success as both novel and then a play.

The characters of Puccini's *La Bohème* were drawn directly from Murger's *Scènes:* Rodolfo, the poet and writer, was Murger himself, a headstrong and impetuous literary man who described the lives of poor struggling artists. Characteristically, a poet thinks in metaphors and similes, so in Act I of the opera, Rodolfo addresses the stove that does not provide warmth as "an old stove that is idle and lives like a gentlemen of leisure," and when Mimi is reunited with Rodolfo in Act IV, Rodolfo says that she is as "beautiful as the dawn," although Mimi corrects him: "beautiful as a sunset."

Marcello was a figure drawn from several painters whom Murger knew, especially a painter named Tabar who painted "Crossing the Red Sea." In Murger, this "Red Sea" painting was so often rejected by the Louvre that it was joked that if it was put on wheels, it could make the journey from the attic to the committee room of the Louvre and back by itself.

Schaunard is based on the real life Alexandre Schanne who actually called himself Schaunard: he was a sort of Renaissance man: a painter, a writer who actually published his memoirs, and a musician and composer of rather unorthodox symphonies.

Colline, the philosopher, was patterned after a friend they called the "Green Giant," because his oversized green overcoat had four big pockets which they jokingly named after the four main libraries of Paris.

Oddly enough, "bohème" is a word that has a variety of definitions and connotations when it is translated into English. Bohemia is geographically part of the old Czechoslovakian Republic, but bohemian is also the name western Europe once gave to gypsies, presumably to describe their carefree and vagabond life-style. For the Murger/Puccini story, the name applies to the colonies of aspiring and starving young Parisian artists who gathered in the nineteenth century in Montmartre at the time the Church of Sacre Cour was built.

The Bohemia that Murger wrote about is not a place on the map in central Europe, but a place on the edge of bourgeois society. In Murger's Bohemia, the prospective writer, painter, composer, or thinker learns about life, love, suffering, and death, all of which become necessary and important preliminary learning experiences in an artist's development: they provide the artist with an opportunity to grow, evolve, develop, and gain wisdom.

Therefore, bohemian life, as the painter Marcello describes it in Act II, "Oh, sweet age of utopias! You hope and believe, and all seems beautiful," is a time of false illusions. But in the end, the artist must move on and leave the bohemian life before it destroys him, a destruction caused not necessarily by making him freeze or starve, but by arresting him in a world of false dreams and hopes, of promiscuity and rebellion.

In the end, the artist must leave bohemian life and learn discipline: if not, he will ultimately despair and never really learn that first and foremost, it is discipline itself, the antithesis of bohemian life, that is needed to write his poem, or paint his picture.

Ruggiero Leoncavallo also wrote a *La Bohème* based on the same Murger story: Leoncavallo was later to become the composer of the acclaimed *I Pagliacci*, and was earlier part of the original libretto team for Puccini's *Manon Lescaut.*

Attempts were made to persuade both Puccini and Leoncavallo not to write operas simultaneously that were based on Murger's *La Bohème* story: the reason for caution was that the plot was uncomfortably too close to that of Verdi's renowned *La Traviata;* both heroines die of tuberculosis, and in the original Murger, Mimi is persuaded to leave Rodolfo by his wealthy uncle who employs the same arguments posed by Giorgio Germont in *La Traviata.*

The novel was in the public domain, and Ricordi's attempt to secure exclusive rights for Puccini were unsuccessful. As a result, both Puccini and Leoncavallo attacked the work. Initially, a spirited competition developed, but in true operatic tradition, that friendly rivalry eventually turned them into lifelong bitter enemies, particularly after Leoncavallo claimed that he had precedence in the subject.

Leoncavallo's *La Bohème* premiered one year after Puccini's *La Bohème,* and seemed to have been better received. However, today it is rarely performed, having been eclipsed by the more popular Puccini work.

Illica completed the prose scenario, and Giacosa converted the scenario into verse. Initially, the drama was planned as four acts with five scenes: a scene in which Mimi deserts Rodolfo for a rich "Viscontino" was discarded, as well as a scene in the courtyard of Musetta's house after she had been evicted, which Puccini felt bore too much similarity to the mayhem of the Cafe Momus scene.

Puccini was thirty-eight years old when *La Bohème* premiered in 1896. The premiere took place in Turin, Italy, under the baton of a very young conductor named Arturo Toscanini: at that moment, La Scala was under the management of the publisher, Edoardo Sonzogno, who, in revenge against his competitor, made it a point to exclude all Ricordi scores from his repertory.

Most of the critics scathed at Puccini, considering the opera a trivialized work, and far removed from the intense passions he had promised in his earlier *Manon Lescaut.* At *La Bohème*'s world premiere, the eminent music critic, Carlo Bersezio, wrote in the newspaper *La Stampa:* "It hurts me very much to have to say it; but frankly this Bohème is not an artistic success. There is much in the score that is empty and downright infantile. The composer should realize that originality can be obtained perfectly well with the old established means, without recourse to consecutive fifths and a disregard of good harmonic rules. *Bohème* had not made a profound impression on the minds of the audience, and would leave no great trace on the history of the lyric theatre. The composer will do wisely if he writes it off as a momentary mistake. Let him just consider Bohème an accidental error in his artistic career."

In the same vein, *La Bohème* inspired the composer Shostakovich to comment that "Puccini writes marvelous operas, but dreadful music." Another critic advised Puccini to consider *La Bohème* a "momentary error, a brief digression, and to return to the true path of art." And a New York critic called it "summer operatic flotsam and jetsam."

Critics can at times be self-proclaimed soothsayers who seem to be assisted by an infallible crystal ball, and most of the time, they are right. Nevertheless, for *La Bohème,* their prophesies and pontifications about the work's ability to capture the collective minds or hearts of the public turned out to be dead wrong. In particular, they seemed to have belabored the composer's breach and disregard of so-called rules of musical composition like those consecutive fifths that Puccini used so effectively to evoke the gay Christmas celebration in the Latin Quarter of Paris in Act II.

But when the opera was staged in Palermo shortly after its premiere in 1896, the audience was delirious and refused to leave the theater until the final scene had been repeated. Recently, the English critic Frank Granville Barker, reviewing the reissue of the Bjorling-De Los Angeles-Beecham recording, in effect, was explaining how a magical cast can breathe life into Puccini's masterpiece: "The man or woman who is insensitive to the spell of this performance, really isn't fit to live in civilized society, for it is one of the wonders of the world."

The poignancy within the *La Bohème* story itself has become the inspiration for so many other theatrical vehicles. In 1935, Gertrude Lawrence starred in a movie adaptation of *La Bohème* called *Mimi*: Deana Durbin sang "Musetta's Waltz" in the 1940 film "It's a Date"; and Cher, in the film *Moonstruck,* was in effect "lovestruck" after her first encounter with *La Bohème.*

More recently, Jonathan Larse wrote the Pulitzer Prize and Tony Award rock opera *Rent,* a contemporary, or modernized *La Bohème* story depicting young people in their struggles and anxieties: the heroine's tragic death in this story occurs from her addiction to heroin rather than to consumption.

Today, *La Bohème* remains, with *Tosca* and *Madama Butterfly*, one of the central pillars of the Italian repertory. It has become one of the opera world's most popular sentimental favorites, and is among the handful of indispensable operas in the standard repertoire. One can delightfully argue as to which is THE smash hit of opera, *La Bohème, Carmen, La Traviata,* or.......... Audiences have certainly recognized *La Bohème*'s positive virtues and its brilliant theatrical musical ideas, all of which have made the opera universally admired.

One of the fascinations of *La Bohème* lies in its intimate portrait of its characters. In painting, when the plane of the composition is moved forward, the viewer experiences the sensation that he has become more integrated and fused with the scene: he senses a greater presence and a more intimate and emotional closeness to the subject.

Similarly, in this Puccini opera, the intimacy with the characters in the story absorbs the viewer and listener into its time and space: the listener becomes an integral part of this heartwarming and down to earth story; Puccini brilliantly achieves this intimacy with his unquestionable frank emotionalism that explodes from his compelling, romantic, and lush music.

La Bohème is poignantly overpowering entertainment. It is hypnotic and seductive because of its perfect blend and subtle synthesis of humor, joie de vivre, and comedy, all fused with pathos, sentiment, tears, and tragedy.

The bohemian characters serve to overwhelm; like Puccini, one becomes integrated with "his creatures," absorbed in their everyday problems, their dilemmas, their little joys, their loves, and their sorrows. One cannot help but fall in love with all of Puccini's bohemians: Rodolfo the poet, Marcello the painter, Schaunard the musician, Colline the philosopher, Mimi the seamstress, and Musetta the singer.

It is virtually impossible not to identify with these youngsters: these characters all become part of our family. In certain ways they transport us to a time lost in memory, a time of youth, challenges, and dreams, and a whole list of one's own forgotten ambitions, idealisms, aspirations, and hopes.

Their abandon, horseplay, and uninhibited mayhem, are expressions of innocence, insecurity, and all of those fears and anxieties of youth. The bohemians become a reflection of our selves or our family or our children or our grandchildren. Therefore, we empathize with them, and are happy to see them enjoy life and be in love. But when things go wrong, we "feel their pain." When we ultimately witness the cruel fate of Mimi's death, we grieve for Mimi and with the bohemians as if we ourselves have lost a loved one from our family.

These *La Bohème* characters are all part of our collective unconscious: we understand every moment of their youthful anxieties: it is a reminder of our own rite of passage.

*L*a Bohème's simple story, on the surface, brings to life an episode in the lives of four struggling artists, their joys, their sorrows, and their amours. But *La Bohème* has a profound inner meaning and a larger truth when viewed clearly through the operatic microscope: its message is like those in the ancient myths in which a noble transformation evolves from suffering and struggle, or from a sacrifice for the greater good of humanity; consciousness and awareness are raised.

Plato said that you cannot teach philosophy to youth, because they are too caught up in their emotions. For youth, only experiences, pain, difficulty, and even tragedy, can provide that transcendence necessary to develop maturity and understanding: the suffering and struggles of these bohemians serve to represent a "coming of age."

In that sense, the inner meaning of the *La Bohème* story is that it represents a moment of transformation. This chapter in their lives represents a rehearsal for life, in effect, a potent emotional blueprint for the future. Their struggles will transform them; they will lose their innocence; and they will cross a bridge from adolescence into manhood, and in their particular case, a bridge to artistic maturity.

As they experience the trauma in the cruel tragedy of Mimi's death, they grieve and suffer. But those sorrows serve a necessary and useful purpose, because they will develop their inner wisdom and elevate their sensitivities and compassion: as a result, they will mature, become good artists, and learn to create.

In this early episode of their lives depicted in our story, they have learned good fellowship, young love, and humanity. This is the essential understanding of life that will transform their creative and artistic souls upward toward a new and more profound maturity. That transformation becomes a transition that will enable them to find their compass of life, build their confidence, and bring their intuitive creativity to the surface: maturity and growth of the artistic soul is the essence of the *La Bohème* story.

For Puccini, *La Bohème* was a personal story that was biographical: it portrayed many of his own personal experiences. When Puccini was in his twenties and a student at the Conservatory in Milan, he was, like his bohemians in his opera story, a starving young artist.

Pietro Mascagni – later the composer of *Cavalleria Rusticana* – was his roommate. They lived in a garret where they were forbidden to cook, but when they did cook, they sang and played the piano as loud as they could in order to disguise any sounds from their pots and dishes.

They were so poor that they had to pool their pennies to buy a *Parsifal* score in order to study Wagner. Always in deep debt, they supposedly marked a map of Milan with red crosses to show the danger areas where they thought they might run into their creditors.

Puccini, like Colline in Act IV of the opera, once pawned his coat so he could have enough money to take a young ballerina out on the town.

In later life, and after Puccini's phenomenal successes, the bohemian life of his youth became a beautiful and nostalgic memory. Capturing the spirit of his past bohemian lifestyle, Puccini and his cronies formed a club called "La Bohème." It's constitution read:

"The members swear to drink well and eat better...Grumblers, pedants, weak stomachs, fools and puritans shall not be admitted. The Treasurer is empowered to abscond with dues. The President must hinder the Treasurer in the collection of monthly dues. It is prohibited to play cards honestly, silence is strictly prohibited, and cleverness allowed only in exceptional cases. The lighting of the clubroom shall be by means of an oil lamp. Should there be a shortage of oil, it will be replaced by the brilliant wit of the members."

Freud said, "Where psychology leaves off, aesthetics and art begin." And Wagner said, "Art brings the unconscious to consciousness." Puccini's heroines always die, sometimes, brutally and cruelly. An underlying theme present in all of Puccini's operas is that when love is sinful, it is a tragic guilt that must be punished through death.

In Dr. Mosco Carner's biography of Puccini (1958), he hypothesizes a twentieth century psychological interpretation of the inner soul of Puccini himself as he created his pantheon of operatic heroines. Love-death themes were apparently intuitive, unconscious, and compulsive themes for Puccini, all deriving from an unresolved early bondage to his exalted mother image: Puccini had a raging mother complex bordering on an Oedipus Complex.

In Puccini's psyche, the powerful passion of love becomes a tension that is divided into holy, sanctified love, and is opposed by mundane, erotic love. Puccini's love for his exalted mother was sanctified and holy, in effect, his mother-love and mother images were elevated to saintliness. In contrast, erotic and romantic love were sinful: transgressions that must be punished.

Puccini transferred his mother fixations to his heroines. As a result, the sinful loves of Manon, Mimi, Tosca, and Butterfly, become unworthy rivals of the exalted mother image. Each heroine is a manifestation of a social outcast, the inferior woman, and the woman of doubtful virtue: Manon Lescaut is a courtesan, Tosca's love affair with Cavaradossi is immoral, and Mimi lives with Rodolfo in sin.

These women soil Puccini's exalted mother image and as a consequence, he must avenge their guilt and sacrifice, persecute, and eventually destroy them: their death, his unconscious punishment for their sins.

The tragic fate of *La Bohème*'s Mimi fits perfectly within the psychological hypothesis of love as tragic guilt. Mimi pursues erotic and sinful love with Rodolfo, an immorality for which she must be punished through death: with Mimi's death satisfied, Puccini's inner psychological conflicts become resolved. Nevertheless, Mimi is an archetypal Puccinian heroine, so the composer tugs ferociously at the listener's heartstrings as he brilliantly portrays the pathos and agony of her decline.

*L*a Bohème was written during the *fin de siècle*, the end of the nineteenth century, a period starting in 1880 and lasting to about 1910. Nietzsche called the period a time of the "transvaluation of all values," in which man questioned his inner contradictions about the meaning of life and art.

During the eighteenth century Enlightenment, reason was the dominating ideology, and man was considered a rational being who could control the order of his universe and achieve his path to ultimate truth through his power of reason. Reason implied that human progress could be achieved through reform rather than revolution, but the French Revolution, the Reign of Terror, and ultimately, Napoleon, controverted those beliefs, and the backlash to Enlightenment ideology became Romanticism: an explosion of the ideals of freedom and feeling as the path to universal truth.

As the end of the nineteenth century approached, old beliefs about moral and social values had disintegrated and undermined the foundation of the old order of things, eventually giving way to a new age that became spiritually unsettled and self questioning.

Scientific truth and religious faith were in perpetual conflict and tension, a battle that continues today. Traditional values were put into question by the influences of Marx, Darwin, Freud, and in theology, by the German writer, David Strauss: his book, *The Life of Jesus,* was a complete deconstruction of New Testament Divine revelation.

Artistic expression evolved from the sentimentalism and noble ideals of Romanticism, to the portrayal of the savage passions in Realism, or *verismo*, in many respects, the latter expressing *fin de siècle* despair and chaos. Artists during this period looked deeply into man's inner soul, and felt compelled to portray his unconscious fantasies through their art: they probed deeply into the hidden recesses of the mind to convey secrets about neurotic and erotic sensibilities.

Their resultant artistic expression portrayed disillusionment, frustration, and despair. Art proceeded to treat the ugly, physical and mental disease, and even abnormality. In music, a sense of malaise and pessimism was reflected by Puccini, Mahler, and Debussy: they portrayed an angst, a restlessness and helplessness, and a search for the unconscious demon within the self.

The *fin de siècle* introduced new types of heroes and heroines, sometimes neurotic and sometimes deranged: Richard Strauss's *Salome* brought to the operatic stage a sexual pervert who indulges in necrophilism; *Elektra* deals with matricide; Alban Berg's *Wozzeck* deals with sadism; *Lulu* portrays a nymphomaniac whose kisses end in death.

Likewise, Puccini's art mirrors despair, destruction, spells of lethargy, and frustration, and he dutifully reflects his era as well as his own personal neurosis. In *Turandot,* love and hate are torn between sadism and meek submission to the male, and in *Manon Lescaut*, a seductive and perfidious woman is in conflict between reason and emotion, virtue and vice, and the spirit and the flesh.

In *Tosca*, there is a blend of politics, sex, sadism, suicide, murder, and religion, and the entire tragedy springs from Tosca's abnormal, obsessive, and uncontrollable jealousy, all pitted against Scarpia's sadistic erotic obsessions. The intensity of Cavaradossi's lament and final agony becomes even more acute in his "muoio disperato" ("I die in desperation"), the demon of melancholy which haunted Puccini throughout his entire life.

Puccini had a dark side: his frustration, despair, disillusionment, and despondency, all of which are integrated into his operas with almost photographic faithfulness. They represent his unconscious conflicts and personal neuroses, and are dutifully portrayed in his art: they are the underlying themes of all of his art, and the key to understanding the inner meaning in Puccini's operas.

In Puccini's opera, Mimi dies and the curtain falls. Murger tells us on his last page of *Scènes de la vie de Bohème* what happens to our bohemians after Mimi's death. The bohemians leave "la vie de bohème" as they are supposed to, and for better or worse, like all young idealists and counterculture rebels, join the mainstream and establishment.

Murger tells us that Schaunard, the musician, eventually is successful writing popular songs, and, perish the thought, makes tons of money.

Colline, the philosopher, marries a rich society lady, and spends the rest of his life, as Murger says, "eating cake."

Marcello gets his paintings displayed in an exhibition and actually sells one, ironically, to an Englishman whose mistress is the very Musetta whom he had once loved.

Rodolfo gets good reviews for his first book, and is en route to a successful writing career.

The last lines of Murger have Marcello commenting cynically on their artistic successes. Marcello tells Rodolfo: "we're done for my friend, dead and buried. There is nothing left for the two of us but to settle down to steady work." These artists are sadder, but wiser. Their loves, Mimi and Musetta, will always remain with them as beautiful memories of their youth and their bohemian past.

The *bohème* transformation and transition to maturity has succeeded.

Principal Characters in LA BOHÈME

Marcello, a painter	Baritone
Rodolfo, a poet	Tenor
Colline, a philosopher	Bass
Schaunard, a musician	Baritone
Mimi, a seamstress	Soprano
Musetta, a singer	Soprano
Benoit, the landlord	Bass
Alcindoro, a state councillor	Bass
Parpignol, a vendor	Tenor

Students, townspeople, shopkeepers,
street-vendors, soldiers, waiters and children.

TIME: about 1830

PLACE: Paris

Brief Story Synopsis

On Christmas Eve, during the year 1830, Rodolfo, a poet, gazes out of his garret studio at the snow-covered rooftops of Paris while his friend Marcello works on a painting. Both bohemian artists have no money. To provide heat, Rodolfo lights the stove with one of his manuscripts. Two friends arrive: Colline, a philosopher, and Schaunard, a musician, the latter bringing food and wine. Benoit, the landlord, arrives to collect his overdue rent, but in a humorous encounter he is quickly dispatched; the bohemians fill him with wine and proceed to express mock outrage at his amorous encounters.

Marcello, Colline, and Schaunard go off to the Cafe Momus to celebrate, but Rodolfo stays behind to finish a manuscript. His neighbor, Mimi, knocks on the door, seeking help to light her extinguished candle. She is seized by a coughing fit: she faints, and is then revived. Rodolfo and Mimi fall in love.

In front of the Cafe Momus in the Latin Quarter, Rodolfo buys Mimi a bonnet; Colline buys a secondhand overcoat, and Schaunard bargains over the cost of a pipe and horn. Musetta, Marcello's former sweetheart, arrives accompanied by her elderly "protector," Alcindoro. Musetta succeeds in enticing Marcello to return to her and become sweethearts again. While Alcindoro goes off to buy her a pair of new shoes, the bohemians sneak away and join a military parade: Alcindoro returns to find no Musetta, but the bohemians' exorbitant dinner bill.

Mimi and Rodolfo have argued incessantly, and Rodolfo has moved to an inn where Marcello and Musetta reside. Mimi arrives to tell Marcello that Rodolfo's petty jealousies have tormented their love affair, and she begs his help for them to part. When Rodolfo appears, Mimi hides, only to be given away by a fit of coughing. The lovers decide to reunite until spring while Musetta and Marcello are heard quarrelling vociferously.

Back in their garret, Rodolfo and Marcello are bachelors again, nostalgically reminiscing about the wonderful times they shared with their sweethearts. Colline and Schaunard arrive, and all the bohemians rollick and horseplay, temporarily forgetting about their sadness.

Musetta enters to announces that Mimi has arrived, and she is deathly ill. Musetta sends Marcello to sell her earrings for money to buy medicine, get a doctor, and buy a muff to warm Mimi's freezing hands; Colline goes off to sell his coat.

The two lovers, left by themselves, reminisce about their first meeting. While Mimi sleeps, she dies. The grief-stricken Rodolfo becomes shattered as he realizes the terrible loss.

Story Narrative with Music Highlights

ACT I: Christmas Eve. A garret overlooking the snow-covered roofs of Paris.

La Bohème begins without overture or prelude, but its opening music conveys the lighthearted, carefree spirit of the bohemian artists.

Allegro vivace

The young bohemian artists are near-destitute and poverty stricken. It is freezing in the garret because the bohemians have no money for firewood. Marcello, a painter, is huddled near an easel with his painting "Crossing of the Red Sea," a work he never seems to be able to finish; Rodolfo, a poet, tries to work on a manuscript.

Both artists are hungry, cold, and uninspired. Rodolfo stares out of the garret window, and observes that smoke rises from every chimney but their own.

"Nei cieli bigi guardo fumar dai mille comignoli Parigi"

Allegro vivace
RODOLFO

Nei cie-li bi - gi   guardo fumar dai mil - le co - mignoli Pa -ri - gi,
I'm looking at the gray skies of Paris...

The scene is transformed into humor and fuss when the two freezing artists try to figure ways to generate heat from their stove. They ponder their options: burn a chair for firewood, throw in Marcello's painting, or sacrifice an act from Rodolfo's drama.

While Rodolfo's doomed play goes into the flames, Colline, a philosopher, arrives: he comments how quickly the fire died down with Rodolfo's drama, cynically proclaiming that "brevity is a great asset" (literally, "brevity is the soul of wit").

Schaunard, a musician-friend triumphantly arrives with provisions: beef, pastry, wine, tobacco, and firewood.

Schaunard's theme:

Allegro

The ecstatic bohemians horse around in celebration. Schaunard explains that he received money from an eccentric Englishman, who paid him an outrageous sum to play to a neighbor's noisy parrot until it dropped dead: he actually succeeded, not through his music, but by feeding the parrot poisoned parsley.

The landlord, Benoit, arrives to demand his long overdue rent. As a diversion, the bohemians ply him with wine, which, together with flattery, inspires him to boast about his infamous and indiscreet adventures with young girls. The bohemians pretend mock outrage and threaten to reveal his infidelities to his wife: Benoit is thrust out the door, the bohemians' rent payment temporarily deferred.

Marcello, Colline, and Schaunard leave for the Cafe Momus to celebrate Christmas Eve. Rodolfo decides to stay behind so he can finish writing an article.

Alone, Rodolfo is lethargic and unmotivated. As he throws down his pen, he is suddenly interrupted by a timid knock on the door: it is his beautiful and fragile neighbor, Mimi, exhausted and out of breath from climbing the stairs. Mimi's candle had extinguished from the hallway drafts, and she seeks light to find her way.

Mimi's coughing indicates that she is ill. Both become nervous and fidgety: a candle blows out, a candle is relit, and then the candle blows out again. Mimi faints, and Rodolfo revives her with sprinkles of water and sips of wine.

Just before Mimi is about to leave, she accidentally drops her key, and both grope for the key in the dark. Rodolfo finds the key, and slyly places it into his pocket. Their hands meet in the dark, and Rodolfo tells Mimi: "Che gelida manina se la lasci riscaldar" ("How cold your little hand is! Let me warm it for you.")

Rodolfo has become inspired, and tells Mimi about himself: he is a poor poet, but with his rhymes, dreams, and visions, he has the soul of a millionaire.

"Che gelida manina"
Andantino affetuoso
RODOLFO

Che   ge - li - da   ma - ni - na,   se la la-sci ris -cal - dar,
How cold your little hand is! Let me warm it for you.

And then Rodolfo envisions a new-found love with Mimi, his words underscored with the sweeping and ecstatic signature music of the opera: "Talor dal mio forziere" ("But two thieves robbed my treasures: a pair of pretty eyes.")

"Talor dal mio forziere"

Con molto espressione
RODOLFO

Ta -lor dal mio for - zi - e`- re,   ruban tutti i gioelli due ladri   gli occhi belli.
But two thieves robbed my treasures: a pair of pretty eyes.

Mimi replies modestly to Rodolfo: "Si, Mi chiamano Mimi" ("Yes. They call me Mimi"), explaining to Rodolfo that she embroiders artificial flowers, and yearns for the real blossoms of spring: flowers that speak of love.

"Si, Mi chiamano Mimi"

Andante lento
MIMI

Sì, Mi chia-ma - no   Mi - mi,   ma il mio no - me è Lu-ci - a.
Yes. They call me Mimi, but my real name is Lucia.

From the street below, Rodolfo's friends call him to hurry up and join them to celebrate Christmas Eve at the Cafe Momus. Rodolfo opens the window, and tells them that he will be along shortly: they should be sure to hold two places for him.

As moonlight envelops them, Rodolfo turns to Mimi, enchanted with her beauty and charm, and together they proclaim their new-found love. Rodolfo begins their rapturous duet with "O soave fanciulla" ("Oh! Gentle young lady"), the music rising ecstatically as both sing "Ah tu sol commandi amor" ("Ah! You alone command love!"), a reprise of the signature music from Rodolfo's biographical aria, "Che gelida manina."

Arm in arm, Mimi and Rodolfo walk out into the night to join their friends at the Cafe Momus.

ACT II: The Latin Quarter and the Cafe Momus

Outside the Cafe Momus, crowds, street hawkers, and waiters create a kaleidoscope of Christmas Eve joy and merriment. Schaunard tries to negotiate the purchase of a pipe and horn, Colline a coat; and Rodolfo appears with Mimi, who now wears a charming pink bonnet that he has just bought for her as a present. They proceed to an outside table at the Cafe Momus where Rodolfo introduces Mimi to his friends:

Questa è Mimi, gaia fiorata"

Allegro moderato
RODOLFO

Questa è Mimi, gaia fiorata. Il suo venir comple - ta   la bella compagnia,
This is Mimi, happy flower girl. Her presence completes our beautiful gathering.

All the bohemians proceed to order themselves a lavish dinner, oblivious to the reality that they have no money to pay.

Marcello suddenly turns gloomy as he hears in the distance the voice of his former sweetheart, Musetta. Musetta, decked in feathers, makes a dashing and noisy entrance on the arm of the state councillor, the old and wealthy "sugar daddy," Alcindoro, whom she orders around unmercifully.

Musetta is the last entry into the bohemian family: she is a singer, volatile, tempestuous, conceited, egotistical, flirtatious, and hungry for adulation, but more importantly, upset that she cannot win back her former lover, Marcello.

As the tumult heightens, Musetta tries to get Marcello's attention, but he pretends to ignore her. Frustrated, Musetta hurls plates, and when that fails, she approaches Marcello, and addresses him directly, using every bit of her irresistible charm.

Musetta sings her famous waltz, a song in which she brags about her own popularity and how men are attracted to her: "Quando m'en vo'" ("When I walk alone through the streets, the people stop to look, and inspect my beauty.") Musetta implores Marcello to return to her, but he continues to ignore her.

Musetta's Waltz: "Quando m'en vo'"
Tempo di Valser lento
MUSETTA

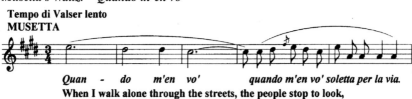

Quan - do   m'en vo'   quando m'en vo' soletta per la via.
When I walk alone through the streets, the people stop to look,

Musetta, now totally baffled and frustrated, pretends that her shoes are pinching her, and sends Alcindoro off to buy her another pair. The moment Alcindoro is gone, she falls into Marcello's arms and suddenly Marcello again becomes seized by Musetta's spell: Marcello capitulates and the lovers are reunited.

A waiter brings the bohemians their staggering check. Unable to pay, Musetta has the waiter add it to Alcindoro's check. As soldiers fill the square and drum their retreat, the four bohemian artists, joined by Mimi and Musetta, follow the parade and disappear into the crowd.

Alcindoro returns with Musetta's new shoes, only to find an immense bill: jilted and abandoned, he drops helplessly into a chair.

ACT III: *The Barrièr d'Enfer, the city gates on the snowy outskirts of Paris*

Act III represents a dramatic transition from the preceding gaiety and abandon of the bohemian artists: the scene portrays the somber and pallid atmosphere of a cold winter's dawn at the customs tollgate at the entrance to the city; gate-keepers admit milkmaids and street cleaners, and from a nearby tavern, the voice of Musetta is heard singing amid sounds of laughter and gaiety.

Marcello and Musetta now live in the tavern. Marcello's "Red Sea" painting has become its signboard: he has found sign painting more profitable than art, and Musetta gives singing lessons.

Mimi appears, shivering, and seized with a nasty coughing fit, she asks a policeman where she can find the painter Marcello. Marcello appears from the tavern, and Mimi proceeds to pour out her desperation to him: Rodolfo has made their love idyll unbearable by exploding into irrational fits of incessant jealousy that have led to constant bickering. Mimi pleads with Marcello to help them to separate.

As Marcello attempts to comfort Mimi, Rodolfo comes out of the tavern. Mimi, in fear of seeing him, hides in the background. She overhears Rodolfo tell Marcello that he wants to separate from his fickle sweetheart, calling her a heartless coquette.

But when Marcello presses Rodolfo for his real reasons, he admits that he truly loves Mimi, but he is terrified that she is dying from her illness, and he feels hopeless because he has no money to care for her.

"Una terribil tosse"

U - na ter-ri-bil tos -se   l'e - sil pet - to   le   scuo - te
A horrible coughing racks her fragile chest.

Mimi overhears Rodolfo and realizes the severity of her illness. Overcome with tears, she rushes to embrace Rodolfo. Mimi insists that they must part for their own good and without regrets. She would be grateful if he would send her her little prayer-book and bracelet, but as a keepsake of their love, she asks him to keep the little pink bonnet he bought her Christmas Eve.

"Addio senza rancor"

Andantino mosso
MIMI

Ad - di - o   sen - za   ran - cor,
Goodbye...no hard feelings,

However, their love is too intense for them to separate, and their intended farewell is transformed into a temporary reconciliation: in a renewed wave of tenderness, they decide to postpone their parting and vow to remain together until springtime.

In a quartet — actually two duets — Mimi's and Rodolfo's music conveys the warmth and tenderness of their love, vividly contrasted against a temperamental quarrel between Marcello and Musetta: Marcello suspects that Musetta has been flirting again, and they furiously hurl insults — and dishes — at each other.

ACT IV: The Bohemians' garret, several weeks later

Rodolfo and Marcello have parted with their respective sweethearts, Mimi and Musetta, and lament their loneliness. They pretend to work, but are uninspired. They tease each other about their ex-lovers: "O Mimi tu più non torni" ("Oh Mimi, you will never return! Oh lovely days!"), a nostalgic reminiscence of their past happiness with their absent amours.

Duet - Rodolfo and Marcello: "Oh Mimi tu più non torni"

Andantino mosso
RODOLFO

O   Mi - mì   tu più non   tor - ni, o gior - ni   bel - li,
Oh Mimi, you will never return! Oh lovely days!

Schaunard and Colline arrive with provisions and the bohemians' spirits become elevated: they dance, horse around, stage a hilarious mock duel, and an imaginary banquet.

Just as their festive mood peaks, they are interrupted by Musetta, who, with great agitation, announces that Mimi is outside: Mimi is deathly sick and they must prepare a bed for her. Mimi felt that the end was near, and she has come to fulfill her wish to die in the arms of her true love, Rodolfo.

Rodolfo and Mimi are reunited, and past quarrels are forgotten. Mimi despairs from her illness and complains of the cold. There is no food or wine, so Musetta gives Marcello her earrings to pawn so they can pay for food, medicine, and a doctor; Colline decides to pawn his treasured overcoat and bids it a touching farewell.

"Vecchia zimarra"

Allegretto moderato e triste
COLLINE

Vecchia zimarra, senti, io resto al pian, tu ascendere il sacro monte or devi. Le mie grazie ricevi.
Listen, my venerable coat, I'm staying behind, but you go on to greater heights. I thank you.

Mimi and Rodolfo are left alone and poignantly reminisce of their first meeting,

Sono andati

Andante calmo
MIMI

Sono and - a - ti? Fingevo di dormire   perchè   volli con te so-la   restare.
Have they gone? I pretended to sleep to make them leave us alone.

Mimi falls off to sleep. Marcello returns with medicine, and Musetta prays for Mimi while Rodolfo lowers the blinds to soften the light.

Schaunard looks toward Mimi, and realizes that she has died. Rodolfo glances at his friends, and senses the tragic truth. Marcello embraces his friend, and urges him to have courage.

Rodolfo falls on Mimi's lifeless body as a thunderous, anguished orchestral fortissimo accompanies his despairing and wrenching cries of grief and loss: "Mimi, Mimi, Mimi."

LA BOHÈME

Libretto

ACT I

A garret: A large window through which the snow-covered roofs of Paris are seen.
There is a a painter's easel with a half finished canvas, a stove, a table, a bed,
four chairs, and books and manuscripts strewn everywhere.
Rodolfo is thoughtful as he looks out the window. Marcello works at his painting, "The
Crossing of the Red Sea," his hands stiff from the cold.
He tries in vain to warm them by blowing on them.

Allegro vivace

Marcello:
Questo "Mar Rosso" mi ammollisce e assidera
com e se addosso mi piovesse in stille.
Pervendarmi affogo un Faraone.

Che fai?

Marcello:(*Seated and continuing to paint*).
This "Red Sea" of mine makes me feel cold and numb
as if it were pouring over me.
In revenge, I'll drown a Pharaoh.
(*To Rodolfo*)
What are you doing?

Allegro vivace
RODOLFO

Nei cie-li bi - gi guardo fumar dai mil - le co - mignoli Pa -ri - gi,

Rodolfo:
Nei cieli bigi guardo fumar dai mille comignoli Parigi,

Rodolfo:
I'm looking at the grey skies of Paris where smoke comes from a thousand chimneys,

e penso quel poltone d'un vecchio
caminetta ingannatore che vive in ozio
come un gran signor.

Marcello:
Le sue redite oneste da un pezzo non
riceve.

Rodolfo:
Quelle sciocche foreste che fan sotto la
neve?

Marcello:
Rodolfo, io voglio dirti un mio pensier
profondo: ho un freddo cane.

Rodolfo:
Ed io, Marcel, non ti nascondo che non
credo al sudor della fronte.

Marcello:
Ho ghiacciate le dita quasi ancora le
tenessi immollate, giù in quella gran
ghiacciaia che è il cuore di Musetta.

Rodolfo:
L'amore è un caminetto che sciupa troppo.

Marcello:
...e in fretta!

Rodolfo:
...dove l'uomo è fascina...

Marcello:
...e la donna è l'alare.

Rodolfo:
...l'una brucia in un soffio . . .

Marcello:
...e l'altra sta a guardare.

Rodolfo:
Ma intanto qui si gela.

and I'm thinking of that deceiving old
stove that is idle and lives like a gentleman of leisure.

Marcello:
It's been a long time since he received his
just income.

Rodolfo:
What are those stupid forests doing, all
covered with snow?

Marcello:
Rodolfo, I want to tell you a profound
thought: I'm freezing cold.

Rodolfo:
As for me, Marcello, I'll be frank: I'm not
exactly sweating.

Marcello:
And my fingers are frozen as if I still
were holding them in that enormous
glacier: Musetta's heart.
(Marcello stops painting)

Rodolfo:
Love is a stove that burns too much.

Marcello:
...and too fast!

Rodolfo:
...where the man is the fuel . . .

Marcello:
...and woman the spark . . .

Rodolfo:
..he burns in a moment . . .

Marcello:
...and she stands by watching!

Rodolfo:
Meanwhile, we're freezing in here!

Marcello:
..e si muore d'inedia!

Marcello:
...and dying from starvation!

Rodolfo:
Fuoco ci vuole.

Rodolfo:
We must have a fire.

Marcello:
Aspetta . . . sacrifichiam la sedia!

Marcello: *(seizing a chair)*
Wait . . . we'll sacrifice the chair!

(Rodolfo stops Marcello. Suddenly he has an idea and shouts with joy.)

Rodolfo:
Eureka!

Rodolfo:
Eureka!
(He runs to the table and grabs his voluminous script)

Marcello:
Trovasti?

Marcello:
You've found it?

Rodolfo:
Sì. Aguzza l'ingegno.
L'idea vampi in fiamma.

Rodolfo:
Yes. Sharpen your wits.
Let "thought" burst into flame.

Marcello:
Bruciamo il "Mar Rosso"?

Marcello: *(pointing to his painting)*
Shall we burn the " Red Sea"?

Rodolfo:
No. Puzza la tela dipinta.
Il mio dramma . . .
l'ardente mio dramma ci scaldi.

Rodolfo:
No. Painted canvas smells.
My play . . .
my ardent drama will warm us.

Marcello:
Vuoi leggerlo forse? Mi geli.

Marcello:
Are you going to read it? I'll freeze.

Rodolfo:
No, in cener la carta si sfaldi e l'estro
rivoli ai suoi cieli.
Al secol gran danno minaccia . . .
e Roma in periglio.

Rodolfo:
No, the paper will become ash and genius
will soar back to its heaven.
A serious loss to the age . . .
and Rome is in danger.

Marcello:
Gran cor!

Marcello:
What a noble heart! .

Rodolfo:
A te l'atto primo!

Rodolfo:
Here, take the first act!

Marcello:
Qua.

Marcello:
Here.

Rodolfo:
Straccia.

Rodolfo:
Tear it up.

Marcello:
Accendi.

Marcello:
Light it.

Rodolfo lights part of the manuscript and throws it into the fire. Then both draw their chairs close to the heat and savor its warmth.

Rodolfo e Marcello:
Che lieto baglior.

Rodolfo and Marcello:
What blissful heat!

The door opens and Colline enters, frozen and stamping his feet. He throws some books on the table that are tied with a handkerchief.

Colline:
Già dell'Apocalisse appariscono i segni.
In giorno di Vigilia non si accettano
pegni!

Una fiammata!

Colline:
Signs of the Apocalypse begin to appear.
No pawning allowed on Christmas Eve!
(He interrupts himself in surprise when he sees the fire.)
A fire!

Rodolfo:
Zitto, si dà il mio dramma.

Rodolfo:
Quiet, my play's being given . . .

Marcello:
. . . al fuoco.

Marcello:
. . . to the stove.

Colline:
Lo trove scintillante.

Colline:
I find it scintillating.

Rodolfo:
Vivo.

Rodolfo:
Brilliant.

Marcello:
Ma dura poco.

Marcello:
But it's a little brief.

Rodolfo:
La brevità gran pregio.

Rodolfo:
Brevity is a great asset.

Colline:
Autore, a me la sedia.

Colline:
Your chair, please, Mr. Author.

Marcello:
Questi intermezzi fan morir d' inedia.
Presto!

Marcello:
These intermissions kill you with
boredom. Get on with it!

Rodolfo:
Atto secondo.

Rodolfo:
Act two.

Marcello:
Non far sussurro.

Marcello:
No whispering.

*Rodolfo rips off another part of the manuscript to kindle the fire. Colline takes a chair
and draws himself near to the fire. R
odolfo stands nearby, ready with the remainder of his manuscript.*

Colline:
Pensier profondo!

Colline:
What profound thoughts!

Marcello:
Giusto color!

Marcello:
How colorful!

Rodolfo:
In quell'azzurro guizzo languente sfuma
un'ardente scena d'amor.

Rodolfo:
In that dying blue flame there is an ardent
love-scene vanishing.

Colline:
Scoppietta un foglio.

Colline:
See that page crackle.

Marcello:
Là c'eran baci!

Marcello:
Those were the kisses!

Rodolfo:
Tre atti or voglio d'un colpo udir.

Rodolfo:
I want to hear three acts at once.

Rodolfo throws the rest of the manuscript into the fire.

Colline:
Tal degli audaci l'idea s'integra.

Colline:
And your bold conception is so unified.

Tutti:
Bello in allegra vampa svanir.

All:
Joyous ideas vanish.

They applaud enthusiastically but suddenly the flame dies.

Marcello:
Oh! Dio . . . già s'abbassa la fiamma.

Marcello:
Oh God! The flame is already dying.

Colline:
Che vano, che fragile dramma!

Colline:
So vain, so fragile a drama!

Marcello:
Già scricchiola, increspasi, muor.

Marcello:
It's already curling up to die.

Colline e Marcello:
Abbasso, abbasso l'autore!

Colline and Marcello:
Down with the author!

Two porters enter carrying food, bottles of wine, cigars, and a bundle of wood.
At the sound, the three men shout with joy, and fall upon the provisions.

Rodolfo:
Legna!

Rodolfo:
Wood!

Marcello:
Sigari!

Marcello:
Cigars!

Colline:
Bordò!

Colline:
Bordeaux!

Rodolfo:
Legna!

Rodolfo:
Firewood!

Marcello:
Bordò!

Marcello:
Bordeaux!

Tutti:
Le dovizie d'una fiera il destin ci destinò
..

All:
Destiny provides us with a feast of plenty!

The porters leave. Schaunard, with an air of triumph, throws some coins on the floor.

Schaunard:
La Banca di Francia per voi si sbilancia.

Schaunard:
The Bank of France has gone broke just for you.

Colline:
Raccatta, raccatta!

Colline: *(gathering up coins)*
Pick them up!

Marcello:
Son pezzi di latta!

Marcello: *(incredulously)*
They must be made of tin!

Schaunard:
Sei sordo? . . . sei lippo?
Quest'uomo chi è?

Schaunard:
Are you deaf? Or blind?
Who is this man?

Rodolfo:
Luigi Filippo! M'inchino al mio Re!

Rodolfo:
Louis Philippe! I bow to my king!

Tutti:
Sta Luigi Filippo ai nostri piè!

All:
Louis Philippe is at our feet!

Schaunard tries to relate his adventure, but the others are heedless, all busily placing the provisions on the table and wood in the stove.

Schaundard:
Or vi dirò: quest'oro, o meglio, argento,
ha la sua brava istoria . . .

Schaunard:
Now I'll tell you: this gold, this silver,
has a noble history . . .

Rodolfo:
Riscaldiamo il camino!

Rodolfo:
Let's light the stove!

Colline:
Tanto freddo ha sofferto!

Colline:
It's hard to endure in this cold!

Schaunard:
Un inglese . . . un signor...lord o milord
che sia, volea un musicista . . .

Schaunard:
An Englishman . . . a gentleman . . . a
lord . . . was looking for a musician . . .

Marcello:
Via! Prepariamo la tavola!

Marcello:
Come! Let's set the table!

Schaunard:
Io? Volo!

Schaunard:
And I? I flew to him.

Rodolfo:
L'esca dov'è?

Rodolfo:
Where are the matches?

Colline:
Là.

Colline:
There.

Marcello:
Qua.

Marcello:
Here.

Schaunard:
...e mi presento. M'accetta, gli domando.

Schaunard:
...I introduce myself. He hires me. I ask him.

Colline:
Arrosto freddo.

Colline:
Cold roast beef.

Marcello:
Pasticcio dolce.

Marcello:
Sweet pastry.

Schaunard:
A quando le lezioni?
Risponde: Incominciam . . . guardare!"
e un pappagallo m'addita al primo pian.
Poi soggiunge:
"Voi suonare finchè quello morire!"

Schaunard:
When do the lessons begin?
He replies: "Let's start . . . look!"
and points to a parrot on the first floor.
Then adds:
"You play until that bird dies!"

Rodolfo:
Fulgida folgori la sala splendida!

Rodolfo
The dining room's brilliant!

Marcello:
Ora le candele.

Marcello:
Now the candles.

Schaunard:
E fu così:
suonai tre lunghi dì.
Allora usai l'incanto di mia presenza
bella. Affascinai l'ancella.
Gli propinai prezzemolo!
Lorito allargò l'ali,
Lorito il becco apri,
da Socrate mori!

Schaunard:
And so it went:
I played for three long days.
Then I used my charm, my handsome
figure . . . I won the serving-girl over.
We poisoned a little parsley.
Lorito spread its wings,
Lorito opened its beak, took a piece of
parsley, and died like Socrates!

Colline:
Pasticcio dolce!

Colline:
Sweet pastry!

Marcello:
Mangiar senza tovaglia?

Marcello:
Eating without a tablecloth?

Rodolfo:
No: un'idea!

Rodolfo:
No! I've an idea.
(Rodolfo takes a newspaper)

Marcello e Colline:
II "Costituzional!"

Marcello and Colline:
The "Constitutional"!

Rodolfo:
Ottima carta . . .
Si mangia a si divora un'appendice!

Rodolfo:
Excellent paper . . .
You eat and devour the news!

Colline:
Chi?

Colline: *(to Schaunard)*
Who?

Schaunard:
Il diavolo vi porti tutti quanti . . .
Ed or che fate?
No! queste cibarie sono la salmeria pei dì
futuri tenebrosi e oscuri.
Pranzare in casa il dì della Vigilia mentre
il Quartier Latino le sue vie
addobba di salsiccie e leccornie?
Quando un olezzo di fritelle imbalsama le
vecchie strade? Là le ragazze cantano
contente.

.

Tutti:
La vigilia di Natal!

Schaunard:
Ed han per eco, ognuna uno studente!
Un po' di religione, o miei signori: si
beva in casa, ma si pranzi fuor.

Schaunard:
Go to the devil, all of you . . .
Now what are you doing?
No! These delicacies are the provisions
for dark and gloomy days in the future.
Dine at home on Christmas Eve when the
Latin Quarter has decked its streets with
food?
When the perfume of fritters is wafted
through the ancient streets?
There the girls sing happily.

All:
It's Christmas Eve!

Schaunard
And each has a student echoing her!
Have some religion, gentlemen: we drink
at home, but we dine out.

As they pour wine there is a knock at the door.

Benoit:
Si può?

Marcello:
Chi è là?

Benoit:
Benoit.

Marcello:
Il padrone di casa!

Schaunard:
Uscio sul muso.

Colline:
Non c'è nessuno.

Schaunard:
E chiuso.

Benoit:
Una parola.

Benoit: *(from outside)*
May I come in?

Marcello:
Who's there?

Benoit:
Benoit.

Marcello:
The landlord!

Schaunard:
Bolt the door.

Colline:
Nobody's home.

Schaunard:
It's locked.

Benoit:
Just one word.

Schaunard:
Sola!

Benoit:
Affitto.

Marcello:
Olà. Date una sedia.

Rodolfo:
Presto.

Benoit:
Non occorre, io vorrei . . .

Schaunard:
Segga.

Marcello:
Vuol bere?

Benoit:
Grazie.

Rodolfo e Colline:
Tocchiamo.

Schaunard:
Beva.

Schaunard: *(opens the door)*
Just one!

(Benoit enters and shows a paper.)
Benoit:
Rent.

Marcello:
Here! Give him a chair.

Rodolfo:
Quickly.

Benoit:
Don't bother, I'd like . . .

Schaunard:
Be seated.

Marcello:
Something to drink?

Benoit:
Thank you.

Rodolfo and Colline:
A toast.

Schaunard:
Drink.

Benoit sets down his glass and shows the paper to Marcello.

Benoit:
Questo è l'ultimo trimestre.

Marcello:
E n'ho piacere.

Benoit:
E quindi.

Schaunard:
Ancora un sorso.

Benoit:
Grazie.

Benoit:
This is the bill for three month's rent.

Marcello:
That's fine.

Benoit:
Therefore.

Schaunard:
Another drop.

Benoit:
Thank you.

I Quattro:
Tocchiam.

Benoit:
Grazie.

I Quattro:
Alla sua salute!

Benoit:
A lei ne vengo perchè il trimestre scorso
mi promise.

Marcello:
Promisi ed or mantengo.

Rodolfo:
Che fai?

Schaunard:
Sei pazzo?

Marcello:

Ha visto? Or via, resti un momento in
nostra compagnia.
Dica: quant'anni ha, caro Signor Benoit?

Benoit:
Gli anni? Per carità!

Rodolfo:
Su a giù la nostra età.

Benoit:
Di più, molto di più.

Colline:
Ha detto su a giù.

Marcello:
L'altra sera al Mabil l'han colto in
peccato d'amor.

The Four:
Let's drink.

Benoit:
Thanks.

The Four:
To your health!

Benoit: *(to Marcello again)*
I come to you because last quarter you
promised me.

Marcello:
I promised and I'll pay.
(He points to the money on the table.)

Rodolfo: *(aside to Marcello)*
What are you doing?

Schaunard:
Are you crazy?

Marcello:
(to Benoit, ignoring the others)
You see? Don't go.
Stay with us a moment.
Tell me: how old are you, dear M. Benoit?

Benoit:
My age? Spare me!

Rodolfo:
Your age, more or less.

Benoit:
More, much more.

While they chat, they refill Benoit's empty glass.

Colline
He said more or less.

Marcello
The other evening at the Mabille they
caught him making sinful love.

Benoit:
Io?

Marcello:
Al Mabil l'altra sera l'han colto.
Neghi?

Benoit:
Un caso.

Marcello:
Bella donna!

Benoit:
Ah! molto!

Schaunard poi Rodolfo:
Briccone!

Colline:
Seduttore! Una quercia . . . un cannone!

Rodolfo:
L'uomo ha buon gusto.

Marcello:
Il crin ricciuto e fulvo.
Ei gongolava arzillo e pettoruto.

Benoit:
Son vecchio ma robusto.

Colline, Schaunard, e Rodolfo:
Ei gongolava arzuto e pettorilio.

Marcello:
E a lui cedea la femminil virtù.

Benoit:
Timido in gioventù, ora me ne ripago.
Si sa, è uno svago qualche donnetta
allegra . . . e . . . un po'.Non dico una
balena o un mappamondo, o un viso
tondo da luna piena.Ma magra, proprio
magra, no, poi no! Le donne magre son
grattacapi e spesso, sopracapi, e son piene
di doglie, per esempio,mia moglie . . .

Benoit:
Me?

Marcello:
They caught you at the Mabille the other
evening. Do you deny it?

Benoit:
An accident.

Marcello:
A lovely woman!

Benoit: *(half drunk)*
Ah! Too much!

Schaunard then Rodolfo:
You rascal!

Colline:
Seducer! He's an oak, a ball of fire!

Rodolfo:
He's a man of taste.

Marcello:
With that curly, tawny hair.
How he swaggered, proud and happy!

Benoit:
I'm old but robust.

Colline, Schaunard, and Rodolfo:
How he swaggered, proud and happy!

Marcello:
Feminine virtue gave in to him.

Benoit:
I'm avenging my youthful timidity.
You know, a lovely woman is my hobby .
....a bit .I don't mean like a whale or a
map of the world or a face like a full
moon. But thin, really thin. No!
Thin women are worrisome and often . . .
a nuisance always full of complaints,
for example my wife . . .

Marcello rises, feigning moral indignation. The others do the same.

Marcello:
Quest'uomo ha moglie e sconcie voglie
ha nel cor!

Marcello:
This man has a wife and hides evil desires
in his heart!

Gli Altri:
Orror!

The Others:
Horror!

Rodolfo:
E ammorba, a appesta la nostra onesta
magion.

Rodolfo:
He corrupts and pollutes our respectable
home.

Gli Altri:
Fuor!

Others:
Out with him!

Marcello:
Si abbruci dello zucchero!

Marcello:
Burn some incense!

Colline:
Si discacci il reprobo.

Colline:
Throw out the scoundrel!

Schaunard:
È la morale offesa che vi scaccia!

Schaunard:
Our offended morality expels you!

Benoit:
Io di . . . io di . . .

Benoit:
I said . . . I . . .

Gli Altri:
Silenzio!

The Others:
Silence!

Benoit:
Miei signori . . .

Benoit:
My dear sirs . . .

Gli Altri:
Silenzio . . . via signore . . .
Via di qua!
E buona sera a vostra signoria!
Ah! Ah! Ah!

The Others:
Silence . . . out, sir . . .
Away with you!
And good evening to your lady!
Ha! Ha! Ha!

(Benoit is thrown out.)

Marcello:
Ho pagato il trimestre.

Marcello:
I've paid the rent.

Schaunard:
Al Quartiere Latin ci attende Momus.

Schaunard:
To the Latin Quarter where Momus awaits us.

Marcello:
Viva chi spende!

Schaunard:
Dividiamo il bottin!

Gli Altri:
Dividiam!

Marcello:
Là ci son beltà scese dal cielo.
Or che sei ricco, bada alla decenza!
Orso, ravviati il pelo.

Colline:
Farò la conoscenza la prima volta d'un
barbitonsore. Guidatemi al ridicolo
oltraggio d'un rasoio.

Tutti:
Andiam.

Rodolfo:
Io resto per terminar l'articolo di fondo
del Castoro.

Marcello:
Fa presto.

Rodolfo:
Cinque minuti. Conosco il mestier.

Colline:
T'aspetterem dabbasso dal portier.

Marcello:
Se tardi udrai the coro.

Rodolfo:
Cinque minuti.

Schaunard:
Taglia corta la coda al tuo Castoro.

Marcello:
Long life to him who pays!

Schaunard:
We'll divide my loot!

The Others:
Let's divide!

(They share the coins.)
Marcello: *(giving Colline a mirror)*
There are heavenly beauties there.
Now that you're rich, you must look
presentable. You bear! Trim your fur.

Colline:
I'll make my first acquaintance with a
beard-barber. Lead me to the absurd,
outrageous razor.

All:
Let's go.

Rodolfo:
I must stay to finish my article for the
Beaver.

Marcello:
Do it fast!

Rodolfo:
Five minutes. I know my trade.

Colline:
We'll wait for you downstairs.

Marcello:
You'll hear us if you're late.

Rodolfo:
Five minutes.

Schaunard:
Cut that Beaver's tail short.

(

Rodolfo takes the light and opens the door. The others start down the stairs.

Marcello:
Occhio alla scala. Tienti alla ringhiera.

Marcello: *(from the stairs)*
Watch the stairs. Hold on to the railing.

Rodolfo:
Adagio.

Rodolfo: *(raising the light)*
Go slowly.

.

Colline:
E buio pesto.

Colline:
It's pitch dark.

Schaunard:
Maledetto portier!

Schaunard:
That damn janitor!

Colline:
Accidenti!

Colline:
An accident!

Rodolfo:
Colline, sei morto?

Rodolfo:
Colline, are you dead?

Colline:
Non ancor.

Colline: *(from below)*
Not yet.

Marcello:
Vien presto.

Marcello:
Come soon.

Rodolfo closes the door, sets his light on the table and tries to write.
Uninspired, he tears up the paper and throws the pen down.

Rodolfo:
Non sono in vena.

Chi è là?

Rodolfo:
I'm not inspired.
(There's a timid knock at the door.)
Who's there?

Mimi:
Scusi.

Mimi: *(outside)*
Excuse me.

Rodolfo:
Una donna!

Rodolfo:
A woman!

Mimi:
Di grazia, mi si è spento il lume.

Mimi:
I'm sorry . . . my light has gone out.

Rodolfo:
Ecco.

Rodolfo: *(opening the door)*
Here.

Mimi:

Vorrebbe . . . ?

Rodolfo:
S'accomodi un momento.

Mimi:
Non occorre.

Rodolfo:
La prego, entri.

Si sente male?

Mimi:
No . . . nulla.

Rodolfo:
Impallidisce!

Mimi:
È il respir . . . quelle scale . . .

Mimi:
(appears in the doorway holding the spent candle in her hand and a key)
Would you . . . ?

Rodolfo:
Make yourself comfortable for a moment.

Mimi:
That's not necessary.

Rodolfo:
Please . . . come in.
(Mimi enters, and has a fit of coughing.)
You're not well?

Mimi:
No . . . it's nothing.

Rodolfo:
You're pale!

Mimi
I'm out of breath . . . the stairs . . .

Mimi faints, and Rodolfo catches her and helps her to a chair.
The key and the candlestick fall from her hands.

Rodolfo:
Ed ora come faccio?

Così. Che viso d'ammalata!

Si sente meglio?

Mimi
Sì.

Rodolfo:
Qui c'è tanto freddo. Segga vicino al fuoco.

Aspetti . . . un po' di vino.

Rodolfo:
Now what shall I do?
(He gets some water and sprinkles her face.)
So. How sickly she looks!

(Mimi revives.)
Are you better now?

Mimi:
Yes.

Rodolfo:
It's so cold here. Come and sit by the fire.

(He helps her to a chair by the stove.)
Wait . . . some wine.

Mimi:
Grazie.

Rodolfo:
A lei.

Mimi:
Poco, poco.

Rodolfo:
Così.

Mimi:
Grazie.

Rodolfo:
(Che bella bambina!)

Mimi:
Ora permetta che accenda il lume.
Tutto è passato.

Rodolfo:
Tanta fretta!

Mimi:
Sì.

Grazie. Buona sera.

Rodolfo:
Buona sera.

Mimi:
Oh! sventata, sventata!
la chiave della stanza dove l'ho lasciata?

Rodolfo:
Non stia sull'uscio: il lume vacilla al
vento.

Mimi:
Oh Dio! Torni ad accenderlo.

Mimi:
Thank you.

Rodolfo:
Here.

Mimi:
Just a little.

Rodolfo:
There.

Mimi:
Thank you.

Rodolfo:
(What a beautiful young girl!)

Mimi: *(rising)*
Now, please, relight my candle.
I'm better now.

Rodolfo:
Why such a hurry!

Mimi:
Yes.
(Rodolfo lights her candle.)
Thank you. Good evening.

Rodolfo:
Good evening.

(Mimi leaves, but then reappears at the door.)

Mimi:
Oh! Foolish me!
Where have I left the key to my room?

Rodolfo:
Don't stand at the door: the wind makes
your light flicker.
(Her candle goes out.)

Mimi:
Heavens! Will you relight it?

Rodolfo runs to her with his light, but when he reaches the door,
his candle also goes out. The room is dark.

Rodlfo:
Oh Dio! Anche il mio s'è spento.

Mimi:
Ah! E la chiave ove sarà?

Rodolfo:
Buio pesto!

Mimi:
Disgraziata!

Rodolfo:
Ove sarà?

Mimi:
Importuna è la vicina . . .

Rodolfo:
Ma le pare!

Mimi:
Importuna è la vicina . . .

Rodolfo:
Cosa dice? ma le pare!

Mimi:
Cerchi.

Rodolfo:
Cerco.

Mimi:
Ove sarà?

Rodolfo:
Ah!

Mimi:
L'ha trovata?

Rodolfo:
There . . . Now mine's out, too.

Mimi:
Ah! And where can my key be?

Rodolfo:
Pitch dark!

Mimi:
Unlucky me!

Rodolfo:
Where can it be?

Mimi:
You've an unfortunate neighbor . . .

Rodolfo:
Not at all.

Mimi:
You've an unfortunate neighbor . . .

Rodolfo:
What do you mean? Not at all!

Mimi:
Search for it.

Rodolfo:
I'm searching.

(They search, touching the floor with their hands.)

Mimi:
Where can it be?

Rodolfo:
Ah!
(He finds the key and puts it in his pocket.)

Mimi:
Did you find it?

Rodolfo:
No.

Mimi:
Mi parve . . .

Rodolfo:
In verità!

Mimi:
Cerca?

Rodolfo:
Cerco.

Rodolfo:
No.

Mimi:
I thought . . .

Rodolfo:
Truthfully!

Mimi:
Are you searching?

Rodolfo:
I'm searching for it.

Guided by her voice, Rodolfo pretends to search as he draws closer to her.
Then he grasps her hand.

Mimi:
Ah!

Mimi: *(surprised)*
Ah!

Andantino affetuoso
RODOLFO

Che ge - li - da ma - ni - na,   se la la-sci ris -cal - dar,

Rodolfo:
Che gelida manina!
Se la lasci riscaldar.
Cercar che giova? Al buio non si trova.
Ma per fortuna è una notte di luna,
e qui la luna l'abbiamo vicina.
Aspetti, signorina, le dirò con due parole
chi son, chi son, e che faccio, come vivo.
Vuole?
Chi son? Chi son? Son un poeta.
Che cosa faccio? Scrivo.
E come vivo? Vivo.
In povertà mia lieta scialo da gran signore
rime ed inni d'amore.
Per sogni a per chimere e per castelli in
aria l'anima ho milionaria.

Rodolfo:
How cold your little hand is!
Let me warm it for you.
What's the use of searching? We'll never
find it in the dark. But luckily there's a
moon, and she's our neighbor here.
Just wait, my dear young lady, and
meanwhile I'll tell you in two words who
I am, what I do, and how I live. Shall I?
Who am I? Who am I? I'm a poet.
What do I do? I write.
How do I live? I live.
In my happy poverty I scale to heaven
with my poems and songs of love.
I'm a millionaire in spirit, with hopes,
dreams, and heavenly castles.

Con molto espressione
RODOLFO

Ta -lor dal mio for - zi - e - re, ruban tutti i gioelli due ladri gli occhi belli.

Talor dal mio forziere ruban tutti i gioielli
due ladri: gli occhi belli.
V'entrar con voi pur ora ed i miei sogni
usati, ed i bei sogni miei tosto si dileguar!
Ma il furto non m'accora poichè, poichè
v'ha preso stanza la speranza.

But two thieves robbed my treasures:
a pair of pretty eyes.
They came in with you, and all my past
dreams have vanished.
But the theft doesn't upset me,
because it has filled me with hope.

Or che mi conoscete parlate voi. Deh
parlate. Chi siete? Vi piaccia dir?

Now that you know me, it's your turn to
speak. Who are you? Will you tell me?

Andante lento
MIMI

Sì, Mi chia-ma - no Mi - mi, ma il mio no - me è Lu-ci - a.

Mimi:
Sì. Mi chiamano Mimì, ma il mio nome è
Lucia.
La storia mia è breve. A tela o e seta
ricamo in casa a fuori. Son tranquilla e
lieta,
ed è mio svago far gigli a rose.
Mi piaccion quelle cose che han sì dolce
malia, che parlano d'amor, di primavere,
che parlano di sogni e di chimere,
quelle cose the han nome poesia . . .
Lei m'intende?

Mimi:
Yes. They call me Mimi, but my real
name is Lucia.
My story is brief. I embroider silk and
satin at home or outside. I'm quiet and
happy, and my pastime is making lilies
and roses.
I love all things that have gentle magic,
that talk of love, of spring, of dreams, and
of fairy tales,
those things called poetry . . .
Do you understand me?

Rodolfo:
Sì.

Rodolfo:
Yes.

Mimi
Mi chiamano Mimì. Il perchè non so.
Sola, mi fo il pranzo da me stessa.
Non vado sempre a messa,
ma prego assai il Signor.
Vivo sola, soletta,
là in una bianca cameretta;

Mimi:
They call me Mimi I don't know why.
I live all by myself and I eat alone.
I don't often go to church,
but I like to pray to God.
I live alone, all alone,
in my tiny white room;

guardo sui tetti e in cielo.
Ma quando vien lo sgelo
Il primo sole è mio,
Il primo bacio dell'aprile è mio!
Il primo sole è mio.

I look at the roofs and the sky.
But when spring comes
the sun's first rays are mine.
April's first kiss is mine!
The sun's first rays are mine!

Germoglia in un vaso una rosa,
foglia a foglia l'aspiro.
Così gentil è il profumo d'un fior.
Ma i fior ch'io faccio, ahimè,
i fior ch'io faccio, ahimè non hanno odore.

I breathe the perfume of rose blossoms in
my vase, I breathe its aroma, petal by
petal. So sweet is the flower's perfume.
But the flowers I make, alas, the flowers I
make, alas, alas, have no scent.

Altro di me non le saprei narrare.
Sono la sua vicina che la vien fuori d'ora
a importunare.

What else can I say?
I'm your neighbor, disturbing you at this
importune hour.

Schaunard:
Ehi! Rodolfo!

Schaunard: *(from below)*
Hey! Rodolfo!

Colline:
Rodolfo!

Colline:
Rodolfo!

Marcello:
Olà! Non senti? Lumaca!

Marcello:
Hey! Can't you hear? You slow-coach!

Colline:
Poetucolo!

Colline:
You scribbler!

Schaunard:
Accidenti al pigro!

Schaunard:
To hell with that lazy one!

Rodolfo, impatient, goes to the window to answer his friends.
The moonlight floods the room with light.

Rodolfo:
Scrivo ancora tre righi avolo.

Rodolfo:
I've a few more words to write.

Mimi:
Chi sono?

Mimi: *(inquiring of Rodolfo)*
Who are they?

Rodolfo:
Amici.

Rodolfo:
Friends.

Schaunard:
Sentirai le tue.

Schaunard:
You'll hear about this.

Marcello:
Che te ne fai lì solo?

Marcello:
What are you doing there alone?

Rodolfo:
Non son solo. Siamo in due.
Andate da Momus, tenete il posto.
Ci saremo tosto.

Rodolfo:
I'm not alone. There's two of us.
Go to Momus and get a table.
We'll be there soon.

Marcello, Schaunard e Colline:
Momus, Momus, Momus,
zitti a discreti andiamocene via.
Momus, Momus.
Trovò la poesia.

Marcello, Schaunard and Colline:
Momus, Momus, Momus.
Quietly, discreetly, we're off.
Momus, Momus.
I found poetry at last.

Rodolfo sees Mimi in the moonlight, and he contemplates her ecstatically.

Rodolfo:
O soave fanciulla,
o dolce viso, di mite circonfuso alba
lunar, in te ravviso il sogno ch'io vorrei
sempre sognar!

Rodolfo:
Oh! Gentle young lady,
oh, sweet face bathed in the moonlight.
I see in you the fulfillment of all my
dreams!

Mim:
(Ah, tu sol comandi, amor!)

Mimi:
(Ah! You alone command love!)

Rodolfo:
Fremon già nell'anima le dolcezze
estreme.

Rodolfo:
My soul throbs from your sweet tenderness!

Mimi:
(Tu sol comandi, amore!)

Mimi:
(You alone command love!)

Rodolfo:
Fremon nell'anima dolcezze estreme.....
nel bacio freme amor!

Rodolfo:
My soul throbs from your sweet tenderness,
the kiss of throbbing love!

Mimi:
(Oh! come dolci scendono le sue lusinghe
al core . . . Tu sol comandi, amor!)

Mimi:
(Oh! How his sweet flattery enters my
heart. You alone command love!)

(Rodolfo kisses Mimi.)
No, per pietà!
No, please!

Rodolfo:
Sei mia!

Rodolfo:
You're mine!

Mimi:
V'aspettan gli amici . . .

Rodolfo:
Già mi mandi via?

Mimi:
Vorrei dir . . . ma non oso.

Rodolfo:
Di'.

Mimi:
Se venissi con voi?

Rodolfo:
Che? Mimì! Sarebbe così dolce restar qui.
C'è freddo fuori.

Mimi:
Vi starò vicina!

Rodolfo:
E ai ritorno?

Mimi:
Curioso!

Rodolfo:
Dammi il braccio, o mia piccina . . .

Mimi:
Obbedisco, signor!

Rodolfo:
Che m'ami . . . di' . . .

Mimi:
Io t'amo.

Rodolfo e Mimi:
Amor! Amor! Amor!

Mimi:
Your friends are waiting.

Rodolfo:
You send me away already?

Mimi:
I want to say....but I dare not...

Rodolfo:
Tell me.

Mimi:
If I come with you?

Rodolfo:
What? Mimi! It would be so fine to stay
here. Outside it's cold.

Mimi:
I'll be near you!

Rodolfo:
And when we come back?

Mimi:
Who knows?

Rodolfo:
Give me your arm, my pretty little one . . .

Mimi:
I obey, sir!

Rodolfo:
Tell me you love me!

Mimi:
I love you.

Rodolfo and Mimi: (*as they depart*)
Love! Love! Love!

ACT II

Evening in the Latin Quarter on Christmas Eve. In the square there is the Café Momus and shops of all kinds.
Mimi and Rodolfo move about the crowd. Colline is nearby at a millinery stand.
Schaunard is at a stand testing a pipe and horn.

I Venditori:
Aranci, datteri! Caldi i marroni. Ninnoli, croci. Torroni a caramelle. Fiori alle belle. Oh! la crostata. Panna montata. Fringuelli, passeri. Datteri! Trote! Latte di cocco! Giubbe! Carote!

Hawkers: Oranges, dates! Hot roasted chestnuts! Crosses, knickknacks! Cookies and candies! Flowers for the ladies! Pies for sale with whipped cream! Finches and larks! Dates! Fresh fish! Coconut milk! Skirts! Carrots!

La Folla:
Quanta folla! Che chiasso! Stringiti a me, corriamo. Lisa! Emma!
Date il passo. Emma, quando ti chiamo!
Ancora un altro giro . . .
Pigliam via Mazzarino. Qui mi manca il respiro! Vedi? Il Caffè è vicino.
Oh! Stupendi gioielli! Son gli occhi assai più bellì! Pericolosi esempi la folla oggi ci dà! Era meglio ai miei tempi!
Viva la libertà!

The Crowd:
What a crowd! Such noise! Hold tight!
Let's run! Lisa! Emma!
Make way there! Emma. I'm calling you!
Once more around . . .
We'll take Rue Mazarin. I can't breathe here . . . See? The cafe's right here.
What wonderful jewels! They're like beautiful eyes! This crowd tonight sets a dangerous example! Things were better in my day! Long live freedom!

Al Caffe:
Andiam. Qua, camerier! Presto. Corri. Vien qua. A me. Birra! Un bicchier! Vaniglia. Ratafià. Dunque? Presto! Da ber! Un caffè . . . Presto. Olà . . .

At the Cafe:
Let's go, Here, waiter! Hurry. Run. Come here. My turn. Beer! A glass! Vanilla. Liqueur! Well? Hurry. Drinks! Coffee . . . Quickly. Hey, there . . .

Schaunard:

Schaunard:
(blowing on a horn and producing false notes)
This D is out of tune. How much for the horn and pipe?

Falso questo Re! Pipa a corno quant'è?

Colline:

Colline:
(at the millinery shop where a woman sews an enormous overcoat for him.)
It's a little worn . . .

È un poco usato . . .

Rodolfo:
Andiam.

Rodolfo:
Let's go.

Mimi:
Andiam per la cuffietta?

Mimi:
Are we going to buy the bonnet?

Colline:
Ma è serio e a buon mercato.

Colline:
But it's cheap and dignified.

Rodolfo:
Tienti al mio braccio stretta.

Rodolfo:
Hold tight to my arm.

Mimi:
A te mi stringo.

Mimi:
I'll hold you close.

Mimi and Rodolfo:
Andiam!

Mimi and Rodolfo:
Let's go!
(They go into the millinery shop.)

Marcello:
Io pur mi sento in vena di gridar:
Chi cuol, donnine allegre, un po'
d'amor?

Marcello:
I, too, feel like shouting: which of you
happy girls wants love?

Venditori:
Datteri! Trote! Prugne di Tours!

Hawkers:
Dates! Trout! Plums from Tours!

Marcello:
Facciamo insieme a vendere a
comprar: Io do ad un soldo il
vergine mio cuor.

Marcello:
Let's make a bargain together.
I'll sell my virgin heart for a penny.

Schaunard:
Fra spintoni a gestate accorrendo,
affretta la folla e si diletta nel
provar voglie matte insoddisfatte.

Schaunard:
Pushing and shoving and running, the
crowd hastens to its joys, feeling insane
desires unsatisfied.

Venditori:
Ninnoli! spillette!

Hawkers:
Trinkets! Brooches!

Colline:
Copia rara, anzi unica: la rammatica
Runica.

Colline: *(showing a book)*
A rare find, truly unique: Runic grammar.

Schaunard:
(Uomo onesto!)

Schaunard:
(What an honest fellow!)

Marcello:
A cena!

Marcello:
Let's eat!

Schaunard e Colline:
Rodolfo?

Marcello:
Entrò da una modista.

Rodolfo:
Viene, gli amici aspettano.

Mimi:
Mi sta ben questa cuffietta rosa?

Venditori:
Panna montata! Latte dicocco! Oh! la
crostata! Panna montata!

Al Caffé:
Camerier! Un bicchier! Presto.Olà . . .
Ratafia.

Rodolfo:
Sei bruna e quel color ti dona.

Mimi:
Bel vezzo di corallo.

Rodolfo:
Ho uno zio milionario. Se fa senno il
buon Dio voglio comprarti un vezzo assai
più bel!

Monello, Sartine, Studenti:
Ah! ah! ah! ah!

Borghesi::
Facciam coda alla gente! Ragazze, state
attente! Che chiasso! Quanta folla!
Pigliam via Mazzarino! Io soffoco,
partiamo! Vedi il caffè è vicin! Andiam là,
da Momus! Ah!

Venditori::
Oh! la crostata! Panna montata! Fiori alle
belle! Ninnoli, datteri, caldi i marron!
Fringuelli, passeri, panna,torron!

Schaunard and Colline:
And Rodolfo?

Marcello:
He went into the milliner's.
(Rodolfo and Mimi come out of the shop.)

Rodolfo:
Come, my friends are waiting.

Mimi:
How do you like my pink bonnet?

Hawkers:
Whipped Cream! Coconut milk! Pies!
Whipped cream!

Cafe Customers:
Waiter! A glass! Quick. Hey there . . .
Liqueur.

Rodolfo:
You're dark and that color suits you.

Mimi: *(looking back at the shop)*
That lovely coral necklace.

Rodolfo:
I've a millionaire uncle. If God acts
wisely, I'll buy you a necklace much more
beautiful.

Urchins, Dressmakers, Students:
Ah! Ah! Ah! Ah!

Townspeople:
Let's follow these people! Girls, watch
out! Such noise! What a crowd! We'll take
the Rue Mazarin! I'm stifling, let's go!
See, the cafe's right here! Let's go there,
to Momus! Ah!

Hawkers:
Pies for sale! Whipped cream! Flowers for
the ladies! Knick-Knacks, dates, hot roasted
chestnuts. Finches, larks! Cream cakes!

Rodolfo:
Chi guardi?

Rodolfo:
Whom are you looking at?

Colline:
Odio il profano volgo al par d'Orazio.

Colline:
I hate the vulgar herd as Horace did.

Mimi:
Sei geloso?

Mimi:
Are you jealous?

Rodolfo:
All'uom felice sta il sospetto accanto.

Rodolfo:
The man who's happy must be suspicious too.

Schaunard:
Ed io quando mi sazio vo' abbondanza di spazio.

Schaunard:
And when I'm stuffing myself I want plenty of room about me.

Mimi:
Sei felice?

Mimi:
Are you happy?

Marcello:
Vogliamo una cena prelibata.

Marcello: *(to the waiter)*
We want a prize dinner.

Rodolfo:
Ah, sì. Tanto.

Rodolfo:
Oh yes. Very.

Marcello:
Lesto.

Marcello:
Quickly.

Schaunard:
Per molti.

Schaunard:
And bring plenty.

Rodolfo:
E tu?

Rodolfo:
And you?

Mimi:
Sì, tanto.

Mimi:
Very.

Marcello, Schaunard and Colline sit at a table in front of the cafe.

Studenti:
Là, da Momus!

Students:
There, to Momus!

Sartine:
Andiam! Andiam!

Dressmakers:
Let's go! Let's go!

Marcello, Colline, Schaunard:
Lesto.

Marcello, Colline, Schaunard:
Quickly!

Voce di Parpignol:
Ecco i giocattoli di Parpignol!

Voice of Parpignol: *(in the distance)*
Here come the toys of Parpignol!

Rodolfo:
Due posti!

Rodolfo:
Two places.

Colline:
Finalmente, eccoci qui!

Colline:
Here they are at last!

Allegro moderato
RODOLFO

Questa è Mimì, gaia fiorata. Il suo venir comple - ta   la bella compagnia,

Rodolfo:
Questa è Mimì, gaia fiorata.
Il suo venir completa la bella compagnia.
Perchè . . . perchè son io il poeta;
essa la poesia.
Dal mio cervel sbocciano i canti, dalle
sue dita sbocciano i fior, dall'anime
esultanti sboccia l'amor.

Rodolfo:
This is Mimi, happy flower-girl.
Her presence completes our beautiful
gathering. Because . . . because I am a
poet; and she is poetry itself.
As verses flow from my brain, the flowers
bloom from her fingers, and from souls
united, love blooms.

Marcello:
Dio che concetti rari!

Marcello:
What rare imagery!

Colline:
Digna est intrari.

Colline:
A rare presentation.

Schaunard:
Ingrediat si necessit.

Schaunard:
She passes inspection.

Colline:
Io non do che un accessit.

Colline:
I grant only one access.

Voce di Parpignol:
Ecco i giocattoli di Parpignol!

Voice of Parpignol: *(closer)*
Here come the toys of Parpignol!

Colline:
Salame . . .

Colline:
Salami . . .

Parpignol arrives in the square, pushing a cart covered with frills and flowers.

Ragazzi e Bambine:
Parpignol! Parpignol! Parpignol! . . .
Ecco Parpignol! Parpignol!
Col carretto tutto fior! Ecco Parpignol!
Voglio la tromba, il cavallin! Il tambur,
tamburel . . . voglio il cannon,
voglio il frustin, dei soldati i drappel.

Boys and Children:
Parpignol! Parpignol! Parpignol!
Here is Parpignol!
With his cart all decked with flowers!
Here is Parpignol! I want the horn, the
toy horse! The drum! The tambourine! I
want the cannon; I want the whip, I want
the soldiers trumpet.

Schaunard:
Cervo arrosto.

Schaunard:
Roast venison.

Marcello:
Un tacchineo.

Marcello:
A turkey.

Schaunard:
Vin del Reno!

Schaunard:
Rhine wine!

Colline:
Vin da tavola!

Colline:
Table wine!

Schaunard:
Aragosta senza crosta!

Schaunard:
Shelled lobster!

Madres:
Ah! che razza di furfanti indemoniati,
che ci venite a fare in questo loco?
A casa, a letto! Via, brutti sguaiati, gli
scappellotti vi parranno poco!
A casa! A letto, razza di furfanti, a letto!

Mothers:
What a bunch of naughty rascals! What
are you doing here now?
Go home to bed, you noisy things. Slaps
will be the least you'll get . . . go home to
bed, you bunch of rascals, to bed!

Un Ragazzo:
Vo' la tromba, il cavallin . . .

A Boy:
I want the horn, the toy horse . . .

Rodolfo:
E tu Mimì, che vuoi?

Rodolfo:
What will you have, Mimi?

Mimì:
La crema.

Mimi:
Some custard.

Schaunard:
E gran sfarzo. C'è una dama.

Schaunard:
The best. A lady's with us.

Ragazzi e Bambine:
Viva Parpignol! Il tambur, tamburel!
Dei soldati il drappel!

Children:
Bravo Parpignol! The drums!
The tambourine! A soldiers trumpet!

(The children run off, following Parpignol.)

Marcello:
Signorina Mimì, che dono raro le ha fatto
il suo Rodolfo?

Marcello:
Tell me, Mimi, what rare gift has Rodolfo
given you?

Mimi:
Una cuffietta a pizzi tutta rosa ricamata.
Coi miei capelli bruni ben si fonde.
Da tanto tempo tal cuffietta è cosa desiata
. . . ed egli ha letto quel che il core
asconde Ora colui che legge dentro a un
core sa l'amore . . . ed è lettore.

Mimi:
An embroidered pink bonnet, all with
lace. It goes well with my dark hair.
I've longed for such a bonnet for months .
. . and he read what was hidden in my
heart. Anyone who can read the heart's
secret knows love . . . he's such a reader.

Schaunard:
Esperto professore.

Schaunard:
He's a professor in the subject.

Colline:
Che ha già diplomi e non son armi prime
le sue rime.

Colline:
With diplomas, and his verses are not
those of a beginner.

Schaunard:
Tanto the sembra ver ciò che egli esprime!

Schaunard:
Everything he says seems so expressive.

Marcello:
O bella età d'inganni e d'utopie!
Si crede, spera, a tutto bello appare.

Marcello:
Oh, sweet age of false utopias!
You hope and believe, and all seems beautiful.

Rodolfo:
La più divina delle poesie è quella, amico,
che c'insegna ad amare!

Rodolfo:
The poem most divine, my friend, is what
teaches us to love!

Mimi:
Amare è dolce ancora più del miele!

Mimi:
Love is sweet, sweeter than honey.

Marcello:
Secondo il palato è miele o fiele!

Marcello: *(hearing Musetta)*
That depends: it's honey or gall!

Mimi:
O Dio, l'ho offeso!

Mimi:
Heavens! I've offended him!

Rodolfo:
E in lutto, o mia Mimì.

Schaunard e Colline:
Allegri! e un toast.

Marcello:
Qua del liquor!

Tutti:
E via i pensier, alti i bicchier. Beviam.

Marcello:
Ch'io beva del tossico!

Schaunard, Colline e Rodolfo:
Oh! Musetta!

Marcello:
Essa!

Le Bottegaie:
To'! Lei! Sì! To'! Lei! Musetta!
Siamo in auge! Che toeletta!

Rodolfo:
He's mourning, Mimi!

Schaunard and Colline:
Cheer up! A toast!

Marcello:
Something to drink!

All:
Away with brooding, let's drink..

Marcello: *(seeing Musetta enter laughing)*
I'll drink some poison!

Schaunard, Colline and Rodolfo:
Oh! Musetta!

Marcello:
Her!

The Shopwomen:
What! Her! Yes! Well! Her! Musetta!
We're in awe. What a dress!

Musetta, accompanied by the old and pompous Alcindoro,
sits at another table in front of the café.

Alcindoro:
Come un facchino correr di qua . . . di là .
. No, no, non ci sta . . .

Musetta:
Vien, Lulù!

Alcindoro:
Non ne posso più.

Musetta:
Vien, Lulù.

Schaunard:
Quel brutto coso mi par che sudi!

Alcindoro:
Running like a porter back and forth . . .
No, it's not proper.

Musetta:
(calling to Alcindoro as if he were a dog)
Here, Lulu!

Alcindoro:
I can't take any more.

Musetta:
Come, Lulu.

Schaunard:
That ugly old fool all in a lather!

Alcindoro:
Come? qui fuori? qui?

Musetta:
Siedi, Lulù.

Alcindoro:
Tali nomignoli, prego,serbateli al te per
tu.

Musetta:
Non farmi il Barbablù!

Colline:
È il vizio contegnoso!

Marcello:
Colla casta Susanna.

Mimi:
Essa è pur ben vestita.

Rodolfo:
Gil angeli vanno nudi.

Mimi:
La conosci? Chi è?

Marcello:
Domandatelo a me. Il suo nome è
Musetta cognome "Tentazione"! Per sua
vocazione fa la rosa dei venti; gira a muta
soventi d'amanti a d'amore . . .
E come la civetta è uccello sanguinario;
il suo cibo ordinario è il cuore . . .
mangia il cuore! Per questo io non a te ho più.

Musetta:
(Marcello è là . . . mi vide . . . E non mi
guarda il vile! Quel Schaunard che ride!
Mi fan tutti una bile! Se potessi picchiar,
se potessi graffiar! Ma non ho sotto man
che questo pellican. Aspetta!)
Ehi! Camerier!

Marcello:
Passatemi il ragù.

Alcindoro:
What? Outside? Here?

Musetta:
Sit, Lulu.

Alcindoro:
Those nicknames, please, when we're
alone.

Musetta:
Don't act like Bluebeard!

Colline:
He's evil behind that front!

Marcello:
With the chaste Susanna.

Mimi:
But she's beautifully dressed.

Rodolfo:
Angels go naked.

Mimi
You know her? Who is she?

Marcello:
Ask me that question. Her first name's
Musetta. Her last name's "Temptation."
Her occupation is being a leaf in the wind
. . . always turning, changing her lovers
and her loves . . . Like an owl she's a bird
of prey. Her favorite food is the heart . . .
she devours them! And so I have no heart.

Musetta:
(Marcello's there . . . he saw me . . . but
the coward won't look at me. And that
Schaunard's laughing! They all make me
livid! If I could just hit them, scratch their
eyes out! But I've got this old pelican on
my hands. Just wait!) Waiter!

Marcello: *(hiding his emotion)*
Pass me the stew.

Musetta:
Ehi! Camerier! questo piatto ha una puzza di rifritto!

Musetta:
Hey! Waiter! This plate smells dirty to me! *(throwing the plate on the ground)*

Alcindoro:
No, Musetta, zitto, zitto!

Alcindoro:
No, Musetta! Quiet, now!

Musetta:
(Non si volta.)

Musetta:
(He doesn't look.)

Alcindoro:
Zitto. Zitto, Modi. Garbo.

Alcindoro:
Quiet, now. Manners! Please!

Musetta:
(Ah! Non si volta.)

Musetta:
(He won't look.)

Alcindoro:
A chi parli?

Alcindoro:
To whom are you speaking?

Colline:
Questo pollo è un poema!

Colline:
This chicken is a poem!

Musetta:
(Ora lo batto, lo batto!)

Musetta:
(Now I'll hit him, I'll hit him!)

Alcindoro:
Con chi parli?

Alcindoro:
Who are you talking to?

Musetta:
Al cameriere. Non seccar!

Musetta:
To the waiter. Don't be a bore!

Schaunard:
Il vino è prelibato!

Schaunard:
The wine is excellent.

Musetta:
Voglio fare il mio piacere . . .

Musetta:
I want to do my own pleasures!

Alcindoro:
Parla pian!

Alcindoro:
Lower your voice!

Musetta:
Vo' far quel the mi pare!

Musetta:
I'll do as I please!

Alcindoro:
Parla pian, parla pian!

Alcindoro:
Lower your voice!

Musetta:
Non seccar!

Musetta:
Don't be a bore!

Sartine e Studenti:
Guarda, guarda, chi si vede,
proprio lei, Musetta!
Con quel vecchio che balbetta, proprio
lei, Musetta! Ah! ah! ah! ah!

Dressmakers and Students:
Look, look who it is,
Musetta herself!
With that stuttering old man, it's Musetta
herself! Ha! Ha! Ha! Ha!

Musetta:
(Che sia geloso di questa mummia?)

Musetta:
(But could he be jealous of this mummy?)

Alcindoro:
La convenienza . . . il grado . . . la virtù!

Alcindoro:
Decorum . . . my rank . . . my reputation!

Musetta:
(Vediamo se mi resta tanto poter so lui da
farlo cedere.)

Musetta:
(Let's see if I still have enough power
over him to make him give in.)

Schaunard:
La commedia è stupenda!

Schaunard:
The play is stupendous!

Musetta:
Tu non mi guardi.

Musetta: *(looking at Marcello)*
You're not looking at me.

Alcindoro:
Vedi bene the ordino!

Alcindoro:
Can't you see I'm ordering?

Schaunard:
La commedia è stupenda!

Schaunard:
The play is stupendous!

Colline:
Stupenda!

Colline:
Stupendous!

Rodolfo:
Sappi per tuo governo che non darei
perdono in sempiterno.

Rodolfo: *(to Mimi)*
If you would treat me like that I'd never
forgive you.

Schaunard:
Essa all'un parla perchè l'altro intenda.

Schaunard:
She speaks to one for the other to hear.

Mimi:
Io t'amo tanto, e sono tutta tua . . .
Che mi parli di perdono?

Mimi: *(to Rodolfo)*
I love you so, and I'm all yours . . .
Why speak of forgiveness?

Colline:
E l'altro invan crudel finge di non capir,
ma sugge miel.

Colline: *(to Schaunard)*
And the other is cruel and pretends he is
deaf, but he enjoys it all.

Musetta:
Ma il tuo cuore martella.

Musetta:
But your heart's like a hammer.

Alcindoro:
Parla piano.

Alcindoro:
Lower your voice.

Musetta:
Ma il tuo cuore martella.

Musetta:
But your heart's like a hammer.

Alcindoro:
Piano, piano!

Alcindoro:
Lower your voice.

Tempo di Valser lento
MUSETTA

Quan - do   m'en   vo'   quando m'en vo' soletta per la via.

Musetta:
Quando men'vo soletta per la via,
la gente sosta a mira,
e la bellezza mia tutta ricerca in me,
ricerca in me da capo a piè.

Musetta:
When I walk alone through the streets,
the people stop to look
and inspect my beauty, examining me
from head to toe.

Marcello:
Legatemi alla seggiola!

Marcello:
Tie me to the chair!

Alcindoro:
Quella gente che dirà?

Alcindoro:
What will people say?

Musetta:
Ed assaporo allor la bramo sia sottil che
dagli occhi traspira e dai palesi vezzi
intender sa alle occulte beltà.
Così l'effluvio del desio tutta m'aggira.
Felice mi fa, felice me fa.

Musetta:
And then I savor the subtle longing in
their eyes when they guess at my charms
and mysterious beauty.
A rush of desire surrounds me. It makes
me happy, it makes me happy.

Alcindoro:
(Quel canto scurrile mi muove labile!)

Alcindoro:
(This scurrilous song infuriates me!)

Musetta:
E tu che sai, che memori e ti struggi, da
me tanto rifuggi? So ben: le angoscie tue
non le vuoi dir, ma ti senti morir.

Musetta:
You must remember that you can't escape
from me. I know you won't admit that
you're in torment, but it's in vain.

Mimi:
Io vedo ben che quella poveretta tutta
invaghita di Marcello ell'è!

Mimi:
I can tell that the poor girl is head over
heels in love with Marcello.

Alcindoro:
Quella gente che dirà?

Alcindoro:
What will people say?

Rodolfo:
Marcello un dì l'amò . . .

Rodolfo:
Marcello loved her once . . .

Schaunard:
Ah! Marcello cederà!

Schaunard:
Ah! Marcello will give in!

Rodolfo:
La fraschetta l'abbandonò . . .

Rodolfo:
The flirt abandoned him . . .

Colline:
Chi sa mai quel che avverrà!

Colline:
Who knows what'll happen!

Rodolfo:
. . . per poi darsi a miglior vita.

Rodolfo:
. . . to find a better life.

Schaunard:
Trovan dolce a pari illaccio chi tu tende a
chi ci dà.

Schaunard:
The snare is equally sweet to the hunter
and the hunted.

Colline:
Santi numi! in simil briga mai Colline
intopperà!

Colline:
Gods above! I'd never land myself in
such a situation!

Musetta:
(Ah! Marcello smania... Marcello è
vinto!)

Musetta:
(Ah! Marcello's yearning! Marcello is
conquered!)

Alcindoro:
Parla piano . . . Zitto, zitto!

Alcindoro:
Lower your voice! Be quiet!

Mimi:
Quell'infelice mi muove a pietà.

Mimi:
I feel so sorry for the poor girl.

Colline:
Essa è bella, io non son cieco . . .

Colline:
She's lovely, I'm not blind . . .

Mimi
T'amo!

Mimi: *(nestling close to Rodolfo)*
I love you!

Schaunard:
(Quel bravaccioi a momenti cederà!
Stupenda è la commedia! Marcello
cederà.)

Schaunard:
(The braggart is about to yield!
The play is stupendous! Marcello will give
in!)
(to Colline)

Se una tal vaga persona ti trattasse a tu per
tu, la tua scienza brontolona manderesti a
Belzebù.

If such a pretty person stopped and talked
to you, you'd gladly send all your bearish
philosophy to the devil.

Rodolfo:
Mimì! È fiacco amore quel che le offese
vendicar non sa. Spento amor non risorge.

Rodolfo:
Mimi! Love is weak when wrongs are
unavenged. Love, once dead, cannot be revived.

Mimi:
Quel l' infelice mi muove a pietà.
L'amor ingeneroso è tristo amor!
Quell'infelice.....

Mimi:
I feel so sorry for the poor girl. Love is
sad when it's unforgiving.
I feel so sorry.......

Colline:
Ma piaccionmi assai più una pipa a un
testo greco. Essa è bella, non son cieco....

Colline:
I'm much happier with my pipe and a
Greek text. She's beautiful, I'm not blind....

Alcindoro:
Modi, garbo! Zitto, zitto!

Alcindoro:
Mind your manners! Be quiet!

Musetta:
So ben: le angoscie tue non le vuoi dir.
Ah! ma ti senti morir.

Musetta:
I know: you won't admit your torment.
Ah! But you feel like dying!
(to Alcindoro)

Io voglio fare il mio piacere, voglio far quel
the mi par. Non seccar, non seccar, non seccar!

I'll do as I please, I'll do as I like, don't
be a bore, a bore, a bore!

(Or convience liberarsi del vecchio.)

Ahi!

(Now to get rid of the old man.)
(pretending a pain)
Ouch!

Alcindoro:
Che c'è?

Alcindoro:
What is it?

Musetta:
Qual dolore, qual bruciore!

Musetta:
The pain! The pain!

Alcindoro:
Dove?

Alcindoro:
Where?

Musetta:
A1 piè!

Marcello:
(Gioventù mia, tu non sei morta, nè di tu
è morto il sovvenir . . .
Se to battessi alla mia porta t'andrebbe il
mio core ad aprir!)

Musetta:
Sciogli! slaccia! rompi! straccia!
Te ne imploro. Laggiù c'è un calzolaio.
Corri presto! ne voglio un altro paio.
Ahi! che fitta, maledetta scarpa stretta!
Or la levo . . . eccola qua. Corri, va, corri!
Presto, va, va!

Mimi:
(Io vedo ben: ell'è invaghita di Marcello.)

Rodolfo:
(Io vedo ben: la commedia è stupenda!)

Alcindoro:
Imprudente! Quella gente che dirà?
Ma il mio grado! Vuoi ch'io
comprometta? Aspetta! Musetta! Vo'!

Colline e Schaunard:
(La commedia è stupenda!)

Musetta:
Marcello!

Marcello:
Sirena!

Schaunard:
Siamo all'ultima scena!

Tutti:
Il conto!

Musetta:
My foot!

Marcello: *(thinking about Musetta)*
(My youth, you're still alive, your
memory's not dead . ..
If you came to my door, my heart would
go to open it!)

Musetta: *(to Alcindoro)*
Loosen it! Untie it! Break it! Tear it!
Please! There's a shoemaker nearby. Run
quickly! I want another pair!
Ah, how it pinches, this damn tight shoe!
I'll take it off . . . here it is. Run, go on,
run! Hurry, hurry!

Mimi:
(I can see she's madly in love with Marcello.)

Rodolfo:
(I can see that the play's stupendous!)

Alcindoro:
How unwise! What will people say?
My reputation! Do you want to ruin it?
Wait! Musetta! I'm going!
(He hurries off.)

Colline and Schaunard:
(The play is stupendous!)

Musetta:
Marcello!

Marcello:
Siren!
(They embrace passionately.)

Schaunard:
Here's the finale!
(The waiter brings the bill.)

All:
The bill!

Schaunard:
Così presto?

Colline:
Chi l'ha richiesto?

Schaunard:
Vediam.

Colline e Rodolfo:
Caro!

Rodolfo, Schaunard, Colline:
Fuori il danaro!

Schaunard:
Colline, Rodolfo e tu, Marcel?

Ragazzi:
La Ritirata!

Marcello:
Siamo all'asciutto!

Schaunard:
Come?

Sartini, Studenti:
La Ritirata!

Rodolfo:
Ho trenta soldi in tutto!

Borghesi:
La Ritirata!

Marcello, Schaunard, Colline:
Come? Non ce n'è più?

Schaunard:
Ma il mio tesoro ov'è?

Monelli:
S'avvicinan per di qua?

Schaunard:
So soon?

Colline:
Who asked for it?

Schaunard:
Let's see.

Colline and Rodolfo:
It's high!
(Drums are heard approaching.)

Rodolfo, Schaunard, Colline:
Out with the money!

Schaunard:
Colline, Rodolfo and you, Marcello?

Children:
The Retreat!

Marcello
We're broke!

Schaunard:
What?

Dressmakers, Students:
The Retreat!

Rodolfo:
I've only got thirty sous.

Townspeople:
The Retreat!

Marcello, Schaunard, Colline:
What? There's no more money?

Schaunard:
Where's my treasure?

Urchins:
Are they coming this way?

Musetta:
Il mio conto date a me.

Musetta: *(to the waiter)*
Give me my bill.

Sartine, Studenti:
No! Di là!

Dressmakers, Students:
No! That way!

Monelli:
S'avvicinan per di là!

Urchins:
They're coming that way!

Sartine, Studenti:
Vien di qua!

Dressmakers, Students:
They're coming this way!

Monelli:
No! vien di là!

Urchins:
No, that way!

Musetta:
Bene!

Musetta:
Good!

Borghesi, Venditori:
Largo! largo!

Townspeople, Hawkers:
Make way! Make way!

Ragazzi:
Voglio veder! voglio sentir!

Children:
I want to see! I want to hear!

Musetta:
Presto, sommate quello con questo! . . .
Paga il signorche stava qui con me.

Musetta:
Quick, add these two bills together . . .
The gentleman who was with me will pay.

Mamme:
Lisetta, vuoi tacere? Tonio, la vuoi finire?

Mothers:
Lisetta, please be quiet. Tonio, stop that at once!

Fanciulle:
Mamma, voglio vedere! Papà, voglio
sentire!

Girls:
Mamma, I want to see. Papa, I want to
hear.

Rodolfo, Marcello, Schaunard, Colline:
Paga il signor!

Rodolfo, Marcello, Schaunard, Colline:
The gentleman will pay!

Ragazzi:
Vuò veder la Ritirata!

Children:
I want to see the Retreat!

Mamme:
Vuoi tacer, la vuoi finir!

Mothers:
Please be quiet! Stop that at once!

Sartine:
S'avvicinano di qua!

Dressmakers:
They're coming this way!

Borghesi:
S'avvicinano di là!

Townspeople:
They're coming that way!

Borghesi, Studenti, Venditori:
Sì, di qua!

Townspeople, Students, Hawkers:
Yes, this way!

Monelli:
Come sarà arrivata, la seguiremo al passo.

Urchins:
When it comes by, we'll march with it!

Colline, Schaunard, Marcello:
Paga il signor!

Colline, Schaunard, Marcello:
The gentleman will pay!

Musetta:
E dove s'è seduto, ritrovi il mio saluto!

Musetta:
And here, where we sat, he'll find my greetings!

(putting the bill on the chair.)

Borghesi:
In quel rulliò to senti la patria maestà.

Townspeople:
That drum-roll expresses our country's glory.

Rodolfo, Colline, Schaunard, Marcello:
E dove s'è seduto, ritrovi il suo saluto!

Rodolfo, Colline, Schaunard, Marcello:
And here, where they say, he'll find greetings!

La Folla:
Largo, largo, eccoli qua!

The Crowd:
Make way, make way, here they come!

Monelli:
Ohè! attenti, eccoli qua!

Uurchins:
Hey! Look out, here they are!

Marcello:
Giunge la Ritirata!

Marcello:
The Retreat is arriving!

La Folla:
In fila!

The Crowd:
All in line!

Colline, Marcello:
Che il vecchio non ci veda fuggir colla
sua preda.

Colline, Marcello:
Don't let the old fool see us make off
with his prize.

Rodolfo:
Giunge la Ritirata!

Rodolfo:
The Retreat is arriving!

Marcello, Schaunard, Colline:
Quella folla serrata il nascondiglio appresti!

Marcello, Schaunard, Colline:
We'll hide ourselves in the crowd.

La Folla:
Ecco il tambur maggiore, più fiero d'un antico guerriero! Il tambur maggior!

The Crowd:
Here's the drum-major! Prouder than an ancient warrior! The drum-major!

Mimi, Musetta, Rodolfo, Marcello, Schaunard, Colline:
Lesti! lesti! lesti!

Mimi, Musetta, Rodolfo, Marcello, Schaunard, Colline:
Hurry! Let's run off?

La Folla:
I Zappatori! i Zappatori, olà! Ecco il tambur maggior! Pare un general! La Ritirata è qua! Eccola là! Il bel tambur maggior! La canna d'or, tutto splendor! Che guarda, passa, va!

The Crowd:
The Sappers! The Sappers, hooray! Here's the drum-major! Like a general! The Retreat is here! Here he is, the handsome drum-major! The golden baton, all aglitter! See, he looks at us as he goes past!

Rodolfo, Marcello, Schaunard, Colline:
Viva Musetta! Cuor biricchin! Gloria ed onor, onor a gloria del Quartier Latin!

Rodolfo, Marcello, Schaunard, Colline:
Brava Musetta! Heart of a rogue! Glory and honor, glory and honor of the Latin Quarter!

La Folla:
Tutto splendor! Di Francia è il più bell'uom! Il bel tambur maggior! Eccola là! Che guarda, passa, va!

The Crowd:
All aglitter! The handsomest man in France, the drum-major! Here he is! See, he looks at us as he goes past!

Musetta, with only one shoe, is carried on the shoulders of Marcello and Colline.
All follow the Retreat and disappear.
Alcindoro returns with a new pair of shoes for Musetta. The waiter hands him the bill,
and exasperated, he falls into a chair, bewildered and perplexed.

ACT III

It is February, and snow is everywhere.
It is dawn at the Barriere d'Enfer, the tollgate to the city.

Spazzini:
Ohè, là, le guardie . . . Aprite! Quelli di
Gentilly! Siam gli spazzini. Fiocca la
neve. Ohè, là! Qui s'agghiaccia!

Sweepers:
Hey, there! Guards! Open up! We're the
sweepers from Gentilly. It's snowing.
Hey! We're freezing here!

Undoganiere:
Vengo.

Customs Officer:
I'm coming.

Voci dal Cabaret:
Chi nel ber trovò il piacer nel suo bicchier,
d'una bocca nell'ardor trovò l'amor.

Voices from the Tavern:
Some find pleasure in their cups,
and others in ardent love.

Voce di Musetta:
Ah! Se nel bicchiersta il piacer,
in giovin bocca sta l'amor.

Voice of Musetta:
Ah! Pleasure is in the glass!
Love lies on your lips.

Voci dal Cabaret:
Trallerallè. Eva a Noè.

Voices from the Tavern:
Tra la la la. Eve and Noah.

Voci dal Boulevard:
Hopplà! Hopplà!

Voices from the Highway:
Houp-la! Giddap!

Doganiere:
Son già le lattivendole!

Customs Officer:
Here come the milkmaids!

The gate is opened for milkmaids and peasants with their carts.

Le Lattivendole:
Buon giorno!

Milkmaids:
Good morning!

Le Contadine:
Burro a cacio! Polli ed ova! Voi da the
pane andate? A San Michele. Ci troverem
più tardi? A mezzodì.

Peasant Women:
Butter and cheese! Chickens and eggs!
Which way are you going? To Saint
Michel! Shall we meet later? Yes, at noon.

Mimi enters, and immediately has a fit of coughing.
She then recovers herself, and inquires of the sergerant.

Mimi:
Sa dirmi, scusi, qual è 1;osteria dove un
pittor lavora?

Sergente:
Eccola.

Mimi:
Grazie.

A buona donna, mi fate il favore di
cercarmi il pittore Marcello? Ho da
parlargli. Ho tanta fretta. Ditegli, piano,
che Mimì 1;aspetta.

Sergente:
Ehi, quel paniere!

Doganiere:
Vuoto!

Sergente:
Passi.

Marcello:
Mimi?

Mimi:
Speravo di trovarvi qui.

Marcello:
E ver, Siam qui da un mese di quell'oste
alle spese. Musetta insegna il canto ai
passeggieri. Io pingo quei guerrieri sulla
facciata. È freddo. Entrate.

Mimi:
C'è Rodolfo?

Marcello
Sì.

Mimi:
Non posso entrar. No! No!

Mimi:
Excuse me, where's the tavern where a
painter works?

Sergeant:
There it is.

Mimi:
Thank you.
*(A waitress comes out of the tavern. Mimi
approaches her.)*
Oh, good woman, please . . . be good
enough to find me Marcello, the painter. I
must see him quickly. Tell him softly
Mimi's waiting.

Sergeant: *(to someone coming in)*
Hey! That basket!

Customs Officer:
Empty!

Sergeant:
Let him through.

(Marcello emerges out of the tavern.)
Marcello:
Mimi?

Mimi:
I hoped I'd find you here.

Marcello:
That's right. We've been here a month, at
the host's expense. Musetta teaches the
guests singing. I paint those warriors by
the door there. It's cold. Come inside.

Mimi
Is Rodolfo there?

Marcello:
Yes.

Mimi:
I can't go in. No! No!

Marcello:
Perchè?

Mimi:
O buon Marcello, aiuto! Aiuto!

Marcello:
Cos'è avvenuto?

Mimi:
Rodolfo m'ama ea mi fugge.
Rodolfo si strugge per gelosia.
Un passo, un detto, un vezzo, un fior lo
mettono in sospetto.
Onde corucci ed ire.
Talor la notte fingo di dormire e in me te
sento fisso spiarmi i sogni in viso.
Mi grida ad ogni istante: non fai per me,
ti prendi un altro amante, non fai per me.
Ahimè! In lui parla il rovello, lo so; ma
che rispondergli, Marcello?

Marcello:
Quando s'è come voi non si vive in
compagnia.

Mimi:
Dite bene. Lasciarci conviene. Aiutateci,
aiutateci voi.
Noi s'è provato più volte, ma invano.

Marcello:
Son lieve a Musetta, ella è lieve a me,
perchè ci amiamo in allegria. Canti a risa,
ecco il fior d'invariabile amor!

Mimi:
Dite bene, dite bene. Lasciarci conviene.
Fate voi per il meglio.

Marcello:
Sta ben. Ora lo sveglio.

Mimi:
Dorme?

Marcello:
Why not?

Mimi:
Oh, good Marcello! Help me!

Marcello:
What's happened?

Mimi:
Rodolfo loves me but flees from me.
Rodolfo struggles with his jealousy.
A chance admission, a step, a word, or a
look arouses his suspicions.
And it starts his anger and rage.
Sometimes at night I pretend to sleep, and
I feel his eyes trying to spy on my dreams.
He shouts at me all the time: "You're not
for me. Find another. You're not for me."
Alas! I know he doesn't really mean it,
but what can I answer, Marcello?

Marcello:
When two people are like you two, they
can't live together.

Mimi:
You're right. We should separate.
Help us, help us.
We've tried again and again, but in vain.

Marcello:
I take Musetta lightly, and she behaves
like me. We're both lighthearted. Laughter
and song, the secret of a lasting love.

Mimi:
You're right, you're right. We should
separate. Do your best for us.

Marcello:
All right. I'll wake him up.

Mimi:
Is he sleeping?

Marcello:
E piombato qui un'ora avanti l'alba.
S'assopi sopra una panca. Guardate.

Che tosse!

Mimi:
Da ieri ho l'ossa rotte. Fuggì da me
stanotte dicendomi: è finita. A giorno
sono uscita e me ne venni a questa volta.

Marcello:

Si desta . . . s'alza. Mi cerca. Viene.

Mimi
Ch'ei non mi veda.

Marcello:
Or rincasate, Mimì. Per carità, non fate
scene qua!

Rodolfo:
Marcello. Finalmente. Qui niun ci sente.
Io voglio separarmi da Mimì.

Marcello:
Sei volubil così?

Rodolfo:
Già un'altra volta credetti morto il mio cor.
Ma di quegli occhi azzurri allo splendor
esso è risotto. Ora il tedio l'assale.

Marcello:
E gli vuoi rinnovare il funeral?

Rodolfo:
Per sempre!

Marcello:
He stumbled in here an hour before dawn
and fell asleep on a bench. Look at him . .
.*(Mimi coughs.)*
What a cough!

Mimi:
I've been exhausted since yesterday. He
fled during the night, saying "It's all
over." At dawn I came here to find you,
my friend.

Marcello:
(watching Rodolfo through the window)
He's waking up. He's looking for me . . .
Here he comes.

Mimi:
He mustn't see me.

Marcello:
Go home now, Mimi. For God's sake, no
scenes here.

*(Mimi hides behind a tree as Rodolfo
emerges from the tavern.)*

Rodolfo:
Marcello! At last! No one can hear us
here. I want to leave Mimi.

Marcello:
Are you as fickle as that?

Rodolfo:
Once again I thought my heart was dead.
But it revived at the gleam of her blue
eyes. Now it drive me insane.

Marcello:
And you want to renew it again?

Rodolfo:
Forever!

Marcello:
Cambia metro. Dei pazzi è l'amortetro
che lacrime distilla. Se non ride a sfavilla,
l'amore è fiacco a roco.
Tu sei geloso.

Marcello:
Change your ways! Gloomy love is
madness and brews only tears. If it
doesn't laugh and glow, love has no
strength or voice. Are you jealous?

Rodolfo:
Un poco.

Rodolfo:
A little.

Marcello:
Collerico, lunatico, imbevuto di
pregiudizi, noioso, cocciuto!

Marcello:
You're raving mad, a mass of suspicions,
a boor, a mule!

Mimi:
(Or lo fa incollerire! Me poveretta!)

Mimi:
(He'll make him angry. Poor me!)

Rodolfo:
Mimi è una civetta the frascheggia con tutti.
Un moscardino di Viscontino le fa l'occhio
di triglia. Ella sgonnella a scopre la caviglia,
con un far promettente a lusinghier.

Rodolfo:
Mimi's just a coquette flirting with
everyone. A dandy Viscount eyes her with
longing, and she shows him her ankles,
and lures him with promises.

Marcello:
Lo devo dir? Che non mi sembri sincer.

Marcello:
Must I tell you? You aren't being honest.

Rodolfo:
Ebbene, no. Non lo son. Invan, invan
nascondo la mia vera tortura.
Amo Mimi sovra ogni cosa al mondo. Io
l'amo! Ma ho paura. Mimi è tanto
malata! Ogni dì più declina. La povera
piccina è condannata.

Rodolfo:
All right, then. I'm not. I try in vain to
hide what really torments me.
I love Mimi more than the world. I love
her! But I'm afraid . . . Mimi is terribly
ill, weaker every day. The poor little thing
is doomed.

Marcello:
Mimi?

Marcello:
Mimi?

Mimi:
(Che vuol dire?)

Mimi:
(What does he mean?)

Lento triste
RODOLFO

U - na ter-ri-bil tos -se   l'e - sil pet - to   le   scuo - te

Rodolfo:
Una terribil tosse l'esil petto le scuote.
Già le smunte gote di sangue ha rosse.

Marcello:
Povera Mimi!

Mimi:
(Ahimè, morire?)

Rodolfo:
La mia stanza è una tana squallida.
Il fuoco è spento. V'entra a l'aggira il
vento di tramontana.
Essa canta a sorride e il rimorso m'assale.
Me cagion del fatale mal che l'uccide.

Marcello:
Che far dunque?

Mimi:
(O mia vita! E finita! Ahimè! morir!)

Rodolfo:
Mimì di serra è fiore. Povertà l'ha
sfiorita, per richiamarla in vita non basta
amore.

Marcello:
Poveretta. Povera Mimi! Povera Mimì!

Rodolfo:
Che! Mimi! Tu qui! M'hai sentito?

Marcello:
Ella dunque ascoltava.

Rodolfo:
Facile alla paura, per nulla io m'arrovello.
Vien là nel tepore.

Mimi:
No, quel tanfo mi soffoca.

Rodolfo:
A horrible coughing racks her fragile
chest Her pale cheeks are flushed.

Marcello:
Poor Mimi!

Mimi: *(overhearing)*
(Am I dying? Alas!)

Rodolfo:
My room's like a cave.
The fire has gone out. The wind and the
winter wind roar through it.
She laughs and sings, and I'm seized with
remorse. I'm the cause of her fatal illness.

Marcello:
What's to be done?

Mimi:
(Oh! My life! It's over! Alas! To die!)

Rodolfo:
Mimi's like a flower lacking water and
sun,
love alone won't bring her back to life.

Marcello:
Poor thing. Poor Mimi!
(Rodolfo hears Mimi's sobs and coughs)

Rodolfo:
What, Mimi? You here! You heard me?

Marcello:
She was listening then.

Rodolfo:
I'm easily frightened, worked up over
nothing. Come inside where it's warm.
(He tries to lead her inside.)

Mimi:
No, the heat would suffocate me.

(Musetta's laughter comes from inside.)

Rodolfo:
Ah! Mimi!

Rodolfo:
Ah, Mimi!

Maarcello:
E Musetta che ride. Con chi ride? Ah la civetta! Imparerai.

Marcello:
That's Musetta laughing. And with whom? The flirt! I'll teach her.
(Marcello runs into the tavern.)

Mimi:
Addio.

Mimi: *(to Rodolfo)*
Goodbye.

Rodolfo:
Che! Vai?

Rodolfo:
What? You're going?

Mimi:
Donde lieta uscì al tuo grido d'amore torna sola Mimi. Al solitario nido ritorna un'altra volta a intesser finti fior.

Mimi:
Where I was happy before your love called me. I'm going back alone to my lonely nest to make false flowers.

Andantino mosso
MIMI

Ad - di - o   sen - za   ran - cor,

Addio senza rancor.
Ascolta, ascolta. Le poche robe aduna che lasciai sparse.
Nel mio cassetto stan chiusi quel cerchietto d'or e il libro di preghiere.
Involgi tutto quanto in un grembiale e manderò il portiere . . .
Bada, sotto il guanciale c'è la cuffietta rosa. Se vuoi ... serbarla a ricordo d'amor.
Addio, senza rancor.

Goodbye . . . no hard feelings.
Listen, listen. Gather up the few things I've left behind.
In the trunk there's the little bracelet and my prayer book.
Wrap them . . . in an apron and I'll send someone for them . . .
Wait! Under the pillow there's my pink bonnet. If you want . . . keep it in memory of our love. Goodbye, no hard feelings.

Rodolfo:
Dunque è proprio finita. Te ne vai, la mia piccina? Addio, sogni d'amor!

Rodolfo:
So it's really over. You're leaving, my little one? Goodbye to our dreams of love.

Mimi:
Addio dolce svegliare alla mattina.

Mimi:
Goodbye to awakening together.

Rodolfo:
Addio sognante vita!

Mimi:
Addio rabuffi a gelosie . . .

Rodolfo:
Che un tuo sorriso acqueta.

Mimi:
Addio sospetti . . .

Rodolfo:
Baci.

Mimi:
Pungenti amarezze . . .

Rodolfo:
Ch'io da vero poeta rimavo con carezze.

Rodolfo e Mimi:
Soli, l'inverno è cosa da morire.

Mimi:
Soli . . .

Rodolfo e Mimi:
Mentre a primavera c'è compagno il sol.

Mimi:
C'è compagno il sol.

Marcello:
Che facevi? Che dicevi?
Presso il foco a quel signore?

Musetta:
Che vuoi dir? Che vuoi dir?

Mimi:
Niuno è solo l'april.

Marcello:
Al mio venire hai mutato di colore.

Rodolfo:
Goodbye to my dream of love.

Mimi:
Goodbye, doubts and jealousies . . .

Rodolfo:
That one smile of yours could dispel.

Mimi:
Goodbye suspicions . . .

Rodolfo:
Kisses.

Mimi:
Poignant bitterness . . .

Rodolfo:
Like a true poet, I made rhymes with caresses.

Rodolfo:
To be alone in winter is death!

Mimi:
Alone . . .

Rodolfo and Mimi:
When springtime returns, the sun will be our friend.

Mimi:
The sun is our companion.
(Marcello and Musetta emerge from the tavern quarrelling.)

Marcello:
What were you doing and saying to that man at the fire?

Musetta:
What do you mean? What do you mean?

Mimi:
Nobody's lonely in April.

Marcello:
When I came in you blushed suddenly.

Musetta:
Quel signore mi deceva . . . "Ama il balla, signorina?"

Rodolfo:
Si parla coi gigli a le rose.

Mimi:
Esce dai nidi un cinguettio gentile.

Marcello:
Vana, frivola civetta!

Musetta:
Arrossendo io rispondevo: "Ballerei sera a mattina."

Marcello:
Quel discorso asconde mire disoneste.

Musetta:
Voglio piena libertà.

Marcello:
Io t'acconcio per le feste . . .

Rodolfo e Mimi:
Al fiorir di primavera c'è compagno il sol.

Musetta:
Che me canti? Che mi gridi? Che mi canti? All'altar non siamo uniti.

Marcello:
Se ti colgo a invicettire! Bada, sotto il mio cappello non ci stan certi ornamenti.

Musetta:
Io detesto quegli amanti che la fanno da mariti.

Rodolfo e Mimi:
Chiacchieran le fontane, la brezza della sera balsami stende sulle doglie umane.

Musetta:
The man was asking me . . "Do you like dancing, Miss?"

Rodolfo:
One can speak with roses and lilies.

Mimi:
Birds twitter softly in their nests.

Marcello:
Vain, empty-headed flirt!

Musetta:
I blushed and answered: "I could dance day and night!"

Marcello:
That speech conceals infamous desires.

Musetta:
I want complete freedom.

Marcello:
I' ll teach you a thing or two . . .

Rodolfo and Mimi:
When springtime returns, the sun will be our friend.

Musetta:
What do you think you're saying? We're not married at the altar.

Marcello:
If I catch you flirting! Keep in mind, there aren't enough horns under my hat.

Musetta:
I can't stand lovers who act just like they're married.

Rodolfo and Mimi:
The whisper of fountains and the evening breeze heals human pain.

Marcello:
Tu non faccio da zimbello ai novizi intraprendenti. Vana, frivola civetta! Ve ne andate? Vi ringrazio, or son ricco divenuto.

Marcello:
I won't be laughed at by some young upstart. Vain, empty-headed flirt! You're leaving? I thank you, I'll be a rich man then.

Musetta:
Fo all'amor con chi mi piace. Non ti garba? Fo all'amor con chi mi piace. Musetta se ne va.

Musetta:
I'll flirt with whom I please. You don't like it? I'll flirt with whom I please. Musetta goes her own way.

Marcello e Musetta:
Vi saluto.

Marcello and Musetta:
Goodbye.

Rodolfo e Mimi:
Vuoi che aspettiam la primavera ancor?

Rodolfo and Mimi:
Shall we wait until spring comes again?

Musetta:
Signor, addio vi dico con piacer!

Musetta:
I bid you, sir, farewell with pleasure!

Marcello:
Son servo a me ne vo!

Marcello:
I'm not your servant!

Musetta:
Pittore da bottega!

Musetta: *(leaving)*
You house-painter!

Marcello:
Vipera!

Musetta:
Viper!

Musetta:
Rospo!

Musetta:
Toad!

Marcello:
Strega!

Marcello: *(reentering the tavern)*
Witch!

Mimi:
Sempre tua . . . per la vita.

Mimi:
Always yours . . . all my life.

Rodolfo e Mimi:
Ci lascieremo alla stagion dei fior!

Rodolfo and Mimi:
We'll part when the flowers bloom!

Mimi:
Vorrei che eterno durasse il verno!

Mimi:
I wish that winter would last forever!

Rodolfo e Mimi:
Ci lascierem alla stagion dei fior!

Rodolfo and Mimi:
We'll part when flowers bloom!

ACT IV

The garret: Marcello is once more working at his easel: Rodolfo writes at a table. Both try to work, but they are uninspired.

Marcello:
In un coupè?

Rodolfo:
Con pariglia e livree. Mi salutò ridendo. Tò Musetta le dissie il cuor? "Non batte o non io sento grazie al velluto che il copre."

Marcello:
Ci ho gusto davver.

Rodolfo:
(Loiola va. Ti rodi e ridi.)

Marcello:
Non batte? Bene. Io pur vidi . . .

Rodolfo:
Musetta?

Marcello:
Mimi.

Rodolfo:
L'hai vista?

Oh guarda!

Marcello:
Era in carrozza vestita come una regina.

Rodolfo:
Evviva. Ne son contento.

Marcello:
(Bugiardo. Si strugge d'amor.)

Marcello:
In a coupè?

Rodolfo:
With footmen and horses. She greeted me laughing. I asked her: "Well! How's your heart? It's not beating or I don't feel it buried so deep in velvet."

Marcello:
I'm happy to hear that.

Rodolfo:
(Faker, you're laughing outside but fretting inside.).

Marcello:
Not beating? Well, I also saw . . .

Rodolfo:
Musetta?

Marcello:
Mimi.

Rodolfo:
You saw her?
(with pretended indifference)
Really?

Marcello:
She was in a carriage dressed like a queen.

Rodolfo:
That's fine. I'm delighted.

Marcello:
(The liar! Love's consuming him.)

Rodolfo:
Lavoriam.

Rodolfo:
Let's get to work.

Marcello:
Lavoriam.

Marcello:
Yes, to work.
(They start working, but quickly throw down brush and pen.)

Rodolfo:
Che penna infame!

Rodolfo:
This pen is terrible!

Marcello:
Che infame pennello!

Marcello:
So is this brush!

Andantino mosso
RODOLFO

O   Mi - mì   tu   più   non   tor - ni,   o   gior - ni   bel - li,

Rodolfo:
(O Mimi, tu piu non torni. O giorni belli,
piccole mani, odorosi capelli, collo di
neve! Ah! Mimì, mia breve gioventù.)

Rodolfo:
(Oh Mimi, you won't return! Oh lovely days!
Those tiny hands, perfumed hair, snowy
neck! Ah! Mimi! My short-lived youth.)

Marcello:
(Io non so come sia cthe il mio pennello
lavori e impasti colori contro voglia mia.
Se pingere mi piace o cielo o terre o
inverni o primavere, egli mi traccia due
pupille nere e una bocca procace, e n'esce
di Musetta il viso ancor.)

Marcello:
(I don't understand how my brush works
and mixes colors to spite me. Whether I
want to paint earth or sky, spring or
winter, the brush outlines two dark eyes
with inviting lips, and Musetta's face
comes out.)

Rodolfo:
(E tu, cuffietta lieve, the sotto il guancial
partendo ascose, tutta sai la nostra
felicità, vien sul mio cor, sul mio cor
morto, poichè è morto amor.)

Rodolfo:
(And you, little pink bonnet that she hid
under the pillow as she left, you know all
of our joy. Come to my heart, console my
lost love.)

Marcello:
(E n'esce di Musetta il viso tutto vezzi a
tutto frode. Musetta intanto gode e il mio
cuor vile la chiama ed aspetta.)

Marcello:
(And that lovely face of Musetta is so
false. Meanwhile Musetta is happy and my
cowardly heart calls her, and waits for her.)

Rodolfo:
Che ora sia?

Rodolfo:
What time is it?

Marcello:
L'ora del pranzo . . . Di ieri.

Marcello:
It's time for dinner . . . Yesterday's dinner.

Rodolfo:
E Schaunard non torna.

Rodolfo:
And Schaunard's not back.
(Schaunard enters and sets four rolls on the table. Colline is with him.)

Schaunard:
Eccoci.

Schaunard:
Here we are.

Rodolfo e Marcello:
Ebbene?

Rodolfo and Marcello:
Well?

Marcello:
Del pan?

Marcello:
Just bread?

Colline:
E un piatto degno di Demostene; un'aringa.

Colline:
A dish worthy of Demosthenes: A herring.

Schaunard:
Salata.

Schaunard:
Salted.

Colline:
Il pranzo è in tavola.

Colline:
Dinner's on the table.
(They sit down.)

Marcello:
Questa è cuccagna da Berlingaccio.

Marcello:
This is like a feast fit for a Caesar.

Schaunard:
Ora to sciampagna mettiamo in ghiaccio.

Schaunard:
(puts the water bottle in Colline's hat)
Now let's put the champagne on ice.

Rodolfo:
Scelga, o Barone, trota o salmone?

Rodolfo:
Which do you choose, Baron, salmon or trout?

Marcello:
Duca, una lingua di pappagallo?

Marcello:
Well, Duke, how about some parrot-tongue?

Schaunard:
Grazie, m'impingua, stasera ho un ballo.

Schaunard:
Thanks, but it's fattening and I must dance this evening.
(Colline rises.)

Rodolfo:
Già sazio?

Colline:
Ho fretta. Il Re m'aspetta.

Marcello:
C'è qualche trama?

Rodolfo, Marcello, Schaunard:
Qualche mister?

Colline:
Il Re mi chiama al minister.

Marcello, Rodolfo, Schaunard:
Bene!

Colline:
Però vedrò . . . Guizot!

Schaunard:
Porgimi il nappo.

Marcello:
Sì, Bevi. Io pappo.

Schaunard:
Mi sia permesso . . . al nobile consesso.

Rodolfo:
Basta.

Marcello:
Fiacco!

Colline:
Che decotto!

Marcello:
Leva il tacco.

Colline:
Dammi il gotto.

Rodolfo:
All finished?

Colline:
I'm in a hurry. The king is waiting for me.

Marcello:
Is there some plot?

Rodolfo, Marcello, Schaunard:
Some mystery?

Colline:
The king has asked me to join his Cabinet.

Marcello, Rodolfo, Schaunard:
Fine!

Colline:
So . . . I'll see Guizot!

Schaunard:
Pass me the goblet.

Marcello:
Here. Drink. I'll eat.

Schaunard:
By the leave . . . of this noble company.

Rodolfo:
Enough!

Marcello:
Idiot!

Colline:
What a concoction!

Marcello:
Stop this nonsense!

Colline:
Give me the goblet!

Schaunard:
M'ispira irresistibile l'estro della romanza. .

Gli Altri:
No!

Schaunard:
Azione coreografica allora?

Gli Altri:
Sì.

Schaunard:
La danza con musica vocale!

Colline:
Si sgombrino le sale. Gavotta.

Marcello:
Minuetto.

Rodolfo:
Pavanella.

Schaunard:
Fandango.

Colline:
Propongo la quadriglia.

Rodolfo:
Mano alle dame.

Colline:
Io detto.

Schaunard:
La lera la lera la!

Rodolfo:
Vezzosa damigella . . .

Marcello:
Rispetti la modestia. La prego.

Schaunard:
I'm irresistibly inspired by romantic expression.

The Others:
No!

Schaunard:
Something choreographic then?

The Others:
Yes.

Schaunard:
Dance with vocal accompaniment!

Colline:
Let the hall be cleared. A gavotte.

Marcello:
Minuet.

Rodolfo:
Pavane.

Schaunard:
Fandango.

Colline:
I propose a quadrille.

Rodolfo:
Take your lady's arm.

Colline:
I'll call the tempo.

Schaunard:
La lera la lera la!

Rodolfo: (*gallantly, to Marcello*)
Lovely maiden . . .

Marcello:
Please, sir, respect my modesty.

Colline:
Balancez.

Colline:
Balancez.

Schaunard:
Prima c'è il Rond.

Schaunard:
The Rondo comes first.

Colline:
No, bestia.

Colline:
No, damn it.

Schaunard:
Che modi da lacchè!

Schaunard:
What boorish manners!

Colline:
Se non erro lei m'oltraggia. Snudi il ferro.

Colline:
You provoke me, I believe. Draw you sword.

Schaunard:
Pronti. Assaggia. Il tuo sangue voglio ber.

Schaunard:
Ready. Lay on. I'll drink your blood.

Colline takes the fire-tongs and Schaunard the poker,
and they act out a   mock sword fight.

Colline:
Un di noi qui si sbudella.

Colline:
One of us will be run through!

Schaunard:
Apprestate una barella.

Schaunard:
Have a stretcher ready!

Colline:
Apprestate un cimiter.

Colline:
And a graveyard too!

Rodolfo e Marcello:
Mentre incalza la tenzone gira a balza
Rigodone.

Rodolfo and Marcello:
While the battle rages, the dancers circle
and leap.
(Musetta enters.)

Marcello:
Musetta!

Marcello:
Musetta!

Musetta:
C'è Mimi .c'è Mimi the mi segue e che sta
male.

Musetta:
Mimi's here, she came with me and she's
ill.

Rodolfo:
Ov'è?

Rodolfo:
Where is she?

Musetta:
Nel far le scale più non si resse.

Musetta:
She couldn't find strength to climb all the stairs.

Rodolfo hastens to Mimi, carries her into the room and places her on the bed.

Rodolfo:
Ah!

Rodolfo:
Ah!

Schaunard:
Noi accostiamo quel lettuccio.

Schaunard:
Let's move the bed closer.

Rodolfo:
Là. Da bere.

Rodolfo:
Here. Something to drink.

Mimi:
Rodolfo.

Mimi:
Rodolfo.

Rodolfo:
Zitta, riposa.

Rodolfo:
Don't speak, rest now.

Mimi:
O mio Rodolfo, mi vuoi qui con te?

Mimi:
Oh my Rodolfo! You want me here with you?

Rodolfo:
Ah, mia Mimi! Sempre, sempre!

Rodolfo:
Ah! My Mimi! Always, always!

Musetta:
Intesi dire che Mimi, fuggita dal Viscontino, era in fin di vita. Dove stia? Cerca, cerca . . . la veggo passar per via, trascinandosi a stento. Mi dice, "Più non reggo . . . Muioi, to sento . . . Voglio morir con lui . . . Forse m'aspetta . . ."

Musetta: *(aside, to the others)*
I heard Mimi fled from the Viscount and was dying. Where was she? I sought her . . Just now I saw her in the street stumbling along. She said; "I can't last long. I know I'm dying . But I want to die with him ... Perhaps he's waiting for me."

Marcello:
Sst!

Marcello:
Sh!

Mimi:
Mi sento assai meglio.

Mimi:
I feel much better.

Musetta:
"M'accompagni, Musetta?"

Musetta:
"Please take me, Musetta?"

Mimi:
Lascia ch'io guardi intorno. Ah, come si sta bene qui. Si rinasce, si rinasce . . . Ancor sento la vita qui. No, tu non mi lasci più.

Mimi:
Let me look around. How wonderful it is here. I'll recover . . . I will . . . I feel life here again. You won't ever leave me.

Rodolfo:
Benedetta bocca, te ancor mi parli.

Musetta:
Che ci avete in casa?

Marcello:
Nulla.

Musetta:
Non caffè? Non vino?

Marcello:
Nulla. Ah! Miseria.

Schaunard:
Fra mezz'ora è morta!

Mimi:
Ho tanto freddo. Se avessi un manicotto!
Queste mie mani riscaldare non si potranno mai?

Rodolfo:
Qui, Nelle mia. Taci. Il parlar ti stanca.

Mimi:
Ho un po' di tosse. Ci sono avvezza.
Buon giorno, Marcello, Schaunard,
Colline, buon giomo.
Tutti qui, tutti qui sorridenti a Mimi.

Rodolfo:
Non parlar, non parlar.

Mimi:
Parlo pian. Non temere. Marcello date
retta: è assai buona Musetta.

Marcello:
Lo so. Lo so.

Musetta:
A te, vendi, riporta qualche cordial.
Manda un dottore!

Rodolfo:
Beloved lips, you speak to me again.

Musetta:
What is there in the house?

Marcello:
Nothing.

Musetta:
No coffee? No wine?

Marcello:
Nothing. Poverty!

Schaunard:
In a half hour she'll be dead!

Mimi:
I'm so cold. If I had a muff? When will
these cold hands of mine get warm again?

Rodolfo:
Here. In mine. Don't speak. Talking will
tire you out.

Mimi:
It's just a little cough. I'm used to it.
Good-day, Marcello, Schaunard, Colline,
good day.
All of you are here, smiling at Mimi.

Rodolfo:
Don't speak, don't speak.

Mimi:
I'll speak softly. Don't fear. Marcello,
believe me Musetta is so good.

Marcello: (*holds Musetta's hand*)
I know. I know.

Musetta: (*gives her earrings to Marcello*)
Here. Sell them. Bring back some cordial
and go for a doctor!

Rodoldo:
Riposa.

Mimi:
Tu non mi lasci?

Roaolfo:
No, no!

Musetta:
Ascolta! Forse è l'ultima volta che ha
espresso un desiderio, poveretta! Pel
manicotto io vo. Con to verrò.

Marcelo:
Sei buona, o mia Musetta.

Rodolfo:
Rest now!

Mimi:
You won't leave me?

Rodolfo:
No! No!

Musetta
Listen! Perhaps it's the poor thing's last
request. I'll get the muff.
I'm coming with you.

Marcello:
How good you are, Musetta.
(Marcello and Musetta exit.)

Allegretto moderato e triste
COLLINE

Vecchia zimarra, senti, io resto al pian, tu ascendere il sacro monte or devi. Le mie grazie ricevi.

Colline:
Vecchia zimarra, senti, io resto al pian, tu
ascendere il sacro monte or devi.
Le mie grazie recevi. Mai non curvasti il
logoro dorso ai ricchi ed ai potenti.
Passar nelle tue tasche come in antri
tranquilli filosofi e poeti.
Ora che i giorni lieti fuggir, ti dico addio,
fedele amico mio. Addio.

Schaunard, ognuno per diversa via
mettiamo insieme due atti di pietà; io . . .
questo! . . . E tu . . . lasciali solilà . . .

Schaunard:
Filosofo, ragioni! E ver . . . Vo Via!

Colline: *(taking off his great coat)*
Listen, my venerable coat, I'm staying
behind, but you go on to greater heights.
I thank you. You never bowed your worn
back to the rich or powerful.
You held in your pockets poets and
philosophers.
Now that those happy times have fled, I
bid you farewell, faithful friend. Farewell.

*(He puts the coat under his arm, then
whispers to Schaunard:)*
Schaunard, each of us can separately
accomplish a kind act.
Let's leave the two of them alone.

Schaunard:
Philosopher, you're right! I'll go.
(They leave.)

Andante calmo
MIMI

Sono and - a - ti? Fingevo di dormire   perchè volli con te so-la restare.

Mimi:
Sono andati?
Fingevo di dormire perchè volli con to
sola restare.
Ho tante cose che ti voglio fire, o una sola
ma grande come il mare,
come il mare profonda ed infinita . . .
sei il mio amor . . . e tutta la mia vita.

Rodolfo:
Ah Mimi, mia bella Mimì!

Mimi:
Son bella ancora?

Rodolfo:
Bella come un'aurora.

Mimi:
Hai sbagliato il raffronto. Volevi dir: bella
come un tramonto. "Mi chiamano Mimì .
. . il perchè non so."

Rodolfo:
Tornò al nido la rondine e cinguetta.

Mimi:
La mia cuffietta! La mia cuffietta!
Ah! te lo rammenti quando sono entrata la
prima volta là?

Rodolfo:
Se lo rammento!

Mimi:
Have they gone?
I pretended to sleep to make them leave
us alone.
I've so many things to tell you, or just
one that is grand like the sea,
as the sea is infinite and profound . . .
so is my love . . . and all my life.

Rodolfo:
Ah! My beautiful Mimi.

Mimi:
Am I still beautiful?

Rodolfo:
Beautiful as the dawn.

Mimi:
You've mistaken the image: you should
have said, beautiful as the sunset. "They
call me Mimi . . . but I don't know why."

Rodolfo:
The swallow comes back to her nest to twitter.
*(He takes the bonnet and places it over
his heart.)*

Mimi:
My bonnet! My bonnet!
Ah! Do you remember when I came in
here the first time?

Rodolfo:
Do I remember!

Mimi:
Il lume s'era spento.

Rodolfo:
Eri tanto turbata.
Poi smarristi la chiave.

Mimi:
E a cercarla tastoni ti sei messo!

Rodolfo:
E cerca, cerca.

Mimi:
Mio bel signorino, posso ben dirlo adesso,
lei la trovò assai presto.

Rodolfo:
Aiutavo il destino.

Mimi:
Era buio e il mio rossor non si vedeva . . .
"Che gelida manina. Se la lasci riscaldar."
Era buio e la man tu mi prendevi.

Rodolfo:
Oh Dio! Mimi!

Schaunard:
Che avvien?

Mimi:
Nulla. Sto bene.

Rodolfo:
Zitta. Per carità.

Mimi:
Sì, sì, perdona. Or sarò buona.

Musetta:
Dorme?

Mimi:
The light had gone out.

Rodolfo:
You were so upset.
Then you lost your key.

Mimi:
And you knelt to hunt for it!

Rodolfo:
I searched and searched.

Mimi:
My dear sir, you might as well admit it,
you found it and hid it quickly.

Rodolfo:
I was helping Fate.

Mimi:
It was dark and you couldn't see me blushing.
"How cold your little hand is .Let me warm it for
you." It was dark and you took my hand in
yours.
(Mimi has another fit of coughing.)

Rodolfo:
Good God! Mimi!
(Schaunard returns.)

Schaunard:
What's wrong?

Mimi:
Nothing. I'm fine.

Rodolfo:
Please . . . don't talk.

Mimi:
Yes, yes forgive me. Now I'll be good.

(Marcello and Musetta return, then Colline.)
Musetta:
Is she sleeping?

Rodolfo:
Riposa.

Rodolfo:
She's resting.

Marcello:
Ho veduto il dottore. Verrà. Gli ho fatto fretta. Ecco il cordial.

Marcello:
I saw the doctor. He's coming. I made him hurry. Here's the cordial.

Mimi:
Chi parla?

Mimi:
Who's speaking?

Musetta:
Io, Musetta.

Musetta: *(handing her the muff)*
Me. Musetta.

Mimi:
O come è bello e morbido! Non più, non più, le mani allividite. Il tepore le abbellirà.
Sei lo che me tu doni?

Mimi:
Oh, how lovely and soft it is. At last, at last, my hands will be warmed and soft.
(to Rodolfo)
Did you do this for me?

Musetta:
Sì.

Musetta:
Yes, he did.

Mimi:
Tu! Spensierato! Grazie. Ma costerà. Piangi? Sto bene. Pianger così perchè? Qui . . . amor . . . sempre con te! Le mani . . . al caldo . . . e dormire......

Mimi:
You spendthrift! Thank you . . . but the cost . . . You're crying? I'm better. Why are you crying like this? Here . . . beloved . . . with you always! My hands . . . the warmth . . . to sleep........

Rodolfo:
Che ha detto il medico?

Rodolfo:
What did the doctor say?

Marcello:
Verrà.

Marcello:
He's coming.

Musetta:
Madonna benedetta, fate la grazia a questa poveretta che non debba morire.

Qui ci vuole un riparo perché la fiamma sventola.

Così. E che possa guarire. Madonna santa, io sono indegna di perdono, mentre invece Mimì è un angelo del cielo.

Musetta: *(praying)*
Oh blessed Mother, be merciful to this poor child who doesn't deserve to die.
(breaking off, to Marcello)
We need shade here; the candle's flickering.

So. Let her get well, Holy Mother, I know I'm unworthy of forgiveness, but Mimi is an angel come down from heaven.

Rodolfo:
Io spero ancora. Vi pare che sia grave?

Rodolfo:
I still have hope. You think it's serious?

Musetta:
Non credo.

Musetta:
I don't think so.
(Schaunard approaches the bed.)

Schaunard:
Marcello, è spirata.

Schaunard: *(softly to Marcello)*
Marcello, she's dead.

Colline:

Musetta, a voi. Come va?

Colline:
(enters and gives money to Musetta)
Here, Musetta. How is she?

Rodolfo:
Vedi, è tranquilla.

Rodolfo:
You see, she's resting.

(Rodolfo becomes aware of the grave expression of the others.)

Che vuol dire? Quell'andare a venire . . .
Quel guardarmi così? . . .

What does this mean? This going back and forth? Why are you looking at me like this?

Marcello:
Coraggio.

Marcello:
Courage.

(Rodolfo runs to the bed.)

Rodolfo:
Mimi! Mimi!

Rodolfo:
Mimi! Mimi!

FINE

END

LA BOHEME

Discography

1928   Torri (Mimi); Giorgini (Rodolfo); Vitulli (Musetta); Badini (Marcello);
        Baracchi (Schaunard); Manfrini (Colline);
        La Scala Chorus and Orchestra;
        Sabajno (Conductor)

1928   Pampanini (Mimi); Marini (Rodolfo); Mirella (Musetta); Vanelli (Marcello);
        Baracchi (Schaunard); Pasero (Colline);
        La Scala Chorus and Orchestra;
        Molajoli (Conudctor)

1938   Albanese (Mimi); Gigli (Rodolfo); Menotti (Musetta); Poli (Marcello);
        Baracchi (Schaunard); Baronti (Colline);
        La Scala Chorus and Orchestra;
        Berrettoni (Conductor)

1946   Albanese (Mimi); Peerce (Rodolfo); McKnight (Musetta);
        Valentino (Marcello); Cehanovsky (Schaunard); Moscona (Colline);
        NBC Symphony and Chorus;
        Toscanini (Conductor)

1947   Sayao (Mimi); Tuckers (Rodolfo); Benzell (Musetta);
        Valentino (Marcello); Cehanovsky (Schaunard); Moscona (Colline);
        Metropolitan Opera Chorus and Orchestra;
        Antonicelli (Conductor)

1950   Tebaldi (Mimi); Prandelli (Rodolfo); Gueden (Musetta); Inghilleri (Marcello);
        Corena (Schaunard); Arié (Colline);
        Academy Santa Cecilia Chorus and Orchestra;
        Eredi (Conductor)

1951   Carteri (Mimi); Tagliavini (Rodolfo); Ramella (Musetta); Taddei (Marcello);
        Latinucci (Schaunard); Siepi (Colline);
        Turin Radio Chorus and Orchestra;
        Santini (Conductor)

1952   Schimenti (Mimi); Lauri-Volpi (Rodolfo); Micheluzzi (Musetta);
        Ciavola (Marcello); Titta (Schaunard); Tatozzi (Colline);
        Rome Opera House Chorus and Orchestra;
        Paoletti (Conductor)

1952   Carteri (Mimi); Tagliavini (Rodolfo); Ramella (Musetta);
        Taddei (Marcello); Latinucci (Schaunard); Siepi (Colline);
        Turin RAI Chorus and Orchestra;
        Santini (Conductor)

1952   Illitsch (Mimi); Delorco (Rodolfo); Boesch (Musetta);
        Baylé (Marcello); Oeggl (Schaunard); Rus (Colline);
        Vienna State Opera Chorus/Austrian Symphony Orchestra;
        Loibner (Conductor)

1956   Los Angeles (Mimi); Björling (Rodolfo); Amara (Musetta);
        Merrill (Marcello); Reardon (Schaunard); Tozzi (Colline); Corena (Benoit);
        RCA Victor Chorus and Orchestra;
        Beecham (Conductor)

1956   Callas (Mimi); Di Stefano (Rodolfo); Moffo (Musetta); Panerai (Marcello);
        Spatafora (Schaunard); Zaccaria (Colline); Badioli (Benoit);
        La Scala Chorus and Orchestra;
        Votto (Conductor)

1957   Stella (Mimi); Poggi (Rodolfo); Rizzoli (Musetta); Capecchi (Marcello);
        Massini (Schaunard); Modesti (Colline); Luise (Benoit); Onesti (Alcindoro);
        San Carlo Opera Chorus and Orchestra;
        Molinaru-Pradelli (Conductor)

1958   Tebaldi (Mimi); Bergonzi (Rodolfo); D'Angelo (Musetta);
        Bastianini (Marcello); Cesari (Schaunard); Siepi (Colline); Corena (Benoit);
        Santa Cecilia Academy Chorus and Orchestra;
        Serafin (Conductor)

1958   Beltrami (Mimi); Antonioli (Rodolfo); Voltriani (Musetta); Testi (Marcello);
        Oppicelli (Schaunard); Ferrein (Colline); Peruzzi (Benoit);
        Bologna State Theatre Chorus/Berlin Radio Orchestra;
        Rigacci (Conductor)

1960   (In German) Lorengar (Mimi); Kónya (Rodolfo); Streich (Musetta);
        Fischer-Dieskau (Marcello); Günther (Schaunard); Bertram (Colline);
        Ollendorf (Benoit);
        Berlin State Opera Chorus and Orchestra;
        Erede (Conductor)

1961   Scotto (Mimi); Poggi (Rodolfo); Meneguzzer (Musetta); Gobbi (Marcello);
        Giorgetti (Schaunard); Modesti (Colline); Carbonari (Benoit);
        Florence Festival Chorus and Orchestra;
        Votto (Conductor)

1961   Moffo (Mimi); Tucker (Rodolfo); Costa (Musetta); Merrill (Marcello);
        Maero (Schaunard); Tozzi (Colline); Corena (Benoit); Onesti (Alcindoro);
        Rome Opera Chorus and Orchestra;
        Leinsdorf (Conductor)

1963   Freni (Mimi); Gedda (Rodolfo); Adani (Musetta); Sereni (Marcello);
        Basiola Jr. (Schaunard); Mazzoli (Colline); Badioli (Benoit);
        Montarsolo (Alcindoro);
        Rome Opera Chorus and Orchestra;
        Schippers (Conductor)

1972   Freni (Mimi); Pavarotti (Rodolfo); Harwood (Musetta); Panerai (Marcello);
        Maffeo (Schaunard); Ghiarov (Colline); Sénéchal (Benoit);
        German Opera Chorus/Berlin Philharmonic Orchestra;
        Von Karajan (Conductor)

1974   Caballé (Mimi); Domingo (Rodolfo); Blegen (Musetta); Milnes (Marcello);
        Sardinero (Schaunard); Raimondi (Colline); Mangin (Benoit);
        Castel (Alcindoro);
        Alldis Choir/London Philharmonic Orchestra;
        Solti (Conductor)

1979   Ricciarelli (Mimi); Carreras (Rodolfo); Putnam (Musetta); Wixell (Marcello);
        Hagegärd (Schaunard); Lloyd (Colline); Van Allan (Benoit);
        Royal Opera House Chorus and Orchestra;
        C. David (Conductor)

1979   Scotto (Mimi); Kraus (Rodolfo); Neblett (Musetta); Milnes (Marcello);
        Manuguerra (Schaunard); Plishka (Colline);
        Ambrosian Opera Chorus/National Philharmonic Orchestra;
        Levine (Conductor)

1987   Hendricks (Mimi); Carreras (Rodolfo); Blasi (Musetta); Quilico (Marcello);
        Cowan (Schaunard); d'Artegna (Colline);
        Chorus and Orchestre National de la RTF;
        Conlon (Conductor)

1988   Réaux (Mimi); Hadley (Rodolfo); Daniels (Musetta); Hampson (Marcello);
        Busterud (Schaunard); Plishka (Colline);
        Academy of Santa Cecilia Chorus and Orchestra;
        Bernstein (Conductor)

1990   Dessì (Mimi); Sabbatini (Rodolfo); Scarabelli (Musetta);
        Gavanelli (Marcello); Antoniozzi (Schaunard); Colombara (Colline);
        Chorus and Orchestra of the Teatro Communale Bologna;
        Gelmetti (Conductor)

LA BOHEME

Videography

Castle VHS
>Cotrubas (Mimi); Shicoff (Rodolfo); Zschau (Musetta);
>Allen (Marcello); Rawnsley (Schaunard); Howell (Colline);
>Orchestra of Royal Opera House/Covent Garden;
>Gardelli (Conductor)
>Copley (DIrector)
>Large (Video Director)

DG VHS
>Freni (Mimi); Raimondi (Rodolfo); Martino (Musetta);
>Panerai (Marcello); Maffeo (Schaunard); Vinco (Colline);
>La Scala Chorus and Orchestra;
>Von Karajan (Conductor);
>A film by Franco Zeffirelli

Virgin VHS
>Freni (Mimi); Pavarotti (Rodolfo); Pacetti (Musetta); Quilico (Marcello);
>Dickson (Schaunard); Ghiarov (Colline);
>San Francisco Opera Chorus and Orchestra;
>Tiziano Severini (Conductor);
>Zambello (Director);
>Large (Video Director)

Decca VHS
>Barker (Mimi); Hobson (Rodolfo); Douglas (Musetta);
>R. Lemke (Marcello); D. Lemke (Schaunard); Rowley (Colline);
>Smith (Conductor);
>Baz Luhrmann (Director);
>Nottage (Video Director)

DICTIONARY OF OPERA AND MUSICAL TERMS

Accelerando - Play the music faster, but gradually.

Adagio - At slow or gliding tempo, not as slow as Largo, but not as fast as Andante.

Agitato - Restless or agitated.

Allegro - At a brisk or lively tempo, faster than Andante but not as fast as Presto.

Andante - A moderately slow, easy-going tempo.

Appoggiatura - An extra or embellishing note preceding a main melodic note or tone. Usually written as a note of smaller size, it shares the time value of the main note.

Arabesque - Flourishes or fancy patterns usually applying to vocal virtuosity.

Aria - A solo song usually structured in a formal pattern. Arias generally convey reflective and introspective thoughts rather than descriptive action.

Arietta - A shortened form of aria.

Arioso - A musical passage or composition having a mixture of free recitative and metrical song.

Arpeggio - Producing the tones of a chord in succession but not simultaneously.

Atonal - Music that is not anchored in traditional musical tonality; it uses the chromatic scale impartially, does not use the diatonic scale and has no keynote or tonal center.

Ballad Opera - 18th century English opera consisting of spoken dialogue and music derived from popular ballad and folksong sources. The most famous is *The Beggar's Opera* which was a satire of the Italian opera seria.

Bar - A vertical line across the stave that divides the music into units.

Baritone - A male singing voice ranging between the bass and tenor.

Baroque - A style of artistic expression prevalent in the 17th century that is marked generally by the use of complex forms, bold ornamentation, and florid decoration. The Baroque period extends from approximately 1600 to 1750 and includes the works of the original creators of modern opera, the Camerata, as well as the later works by Bach and Handel.

Bass - The lowest male voices, usually divided into categories such as:

> **Basso buffo** - A bass voice that specializes in comic roles like Dr. Bartolo in Rossini's *The Barber of Seville*.

> **Basso cantante** - A bass voice that demonstrates melodic singing quality rather than comic or tragic: King Philip in Verdi's *Don Carlos*.

> **Basso profundo** - the deepest, most profound, or most dramatic of bass voices: Sarastro in Mozart's *The Magic Flute*.

Bel canto - Literally "beautiful singing." It originated in Italian opera of the 17th and 18th centuries and stressed beautiful tones produced with ease, clarity, purity, evenness, together with an agile vocal technique and virtuosity. Bel canto flourished in the first half of the 19th century in the works of Rossini, Bellini, and Donizetti.

Cabaletta - Typically a lively bravura extension of an aria or duet that creates a climax. The term is derived from the Italian word "cavallo," or horse: it metaphorically describes a horse galloping to the finish line.

Cadenza - A flourish or brilliant part of an aria commonly inserted just before a finale.

Camerata - A gathering of Florentine writers and musicians between 1590 and 1600 who attempted to recreate what they believed was the ancient Greek theatrical synthesis of drama, music, and stage spectacle; their experimentation led to the creation of the early structural forms of modern opera.

Cantabile - An expression indication urging the singer to sing sweetly.

Cantata - A choral piece generally containing Scriptural narrative texts: Bach Cantatas.

Cantilena - A lyrical melodic line meant to be played or sung "cantabile," or with sweetness and expression.

Canzone - A short, lyrical operatic song usually containing no narrative association with the drama but rather simply reflecting the character's state of mind: Cherubino's "Voi che sapete" in Mozart's *The Marriage of Figaro.* Shorter versions are called canzonettas.

Castrato - A young male singer who was surgically castrated to retain his treble voice.

Cavatina - A short aria popular in the 18th century without the da capo repeat section.

Classical Period - The period between the Baroque and Romantic periods. The Classical period is generally considered to have begun with the birth of Mozart (1756) and ended with Beethoven's death (1830). Stylistically, the music of the period stressed clarity, precision, and rigid structural forms.

Coda - A trailer or tailpiece added on by the composer after the music's natural conclusion.

Coloratura - Literally colored: it refers to a soprano singing in the bel canto tradition with great agility, virtuosity, embellishments and ornamentation: Joan Sutherland singing in Donizetti's *Lucia di Lammermoor.*

Commedia dell'arte - A popular form of dramatic presentation originating in Renaissance Italy in which highly stylized characters were involved in comic plots involving mistaken identities and misunderstandings. The standard characters were Harlequin and Colombine: The "play within a play" in Leoncavallo's *I Pagliacci.*

Comprimario - A singer portraying secondary character roles such as confidantes, servants, and messengers.

Continuo - A bass part (as for a keyboard or stringed instrument) that was used especially in baroque ensemble music; it consists of a succession of bass notes with figures that indicate the required chords. Also called *figured bass, thoroughbass.*

Contralto - The lowest female voice derived from "contra" against, and "alto" voice, a voice between the tenor and mezzo-soprano.

Countertenor, or male alto vocal range - A high male voice generally singing within the female high soprano ranges.

Counterpoint - The combination of one or more independent melodies added into a single harmonic texture in which each retains its linear character: polyphony. The most sophisticated form of counterpoint is the fugue form in which up to 6 to 8 voices are combined, each providing a variation on the basic theme but each retaining its relation to the whole.

Crescendo - A gradual increase in the volume of a musical passage.

Da capo - Literally "from the top": repeat. Early 17th century da capo arias were in the form of A B A, the last A section repeating the first A section.

Deus ex machina - Literally "god out of a machine." A dramatic technique in which a person or thing appears or is introduced suddenly and unexpectedly; it provides a contrived solution to an apparently insoluble dramatic difficulty.

Diatonic - Relating to a major or minor musical scale that comprises intervals of five whole steps and two half steps.

Diminuendo - Gradually getting softer, the opposite of crescendo.

Dissonance - A mingling of discordant sounds that do not harmonize within the diatonic scale.

Diva - Literally a "goddess"; generally refers to a female opera star who either possesses, or pretends to possess, great rank.

Dominant - The fifth tone of the diatonic scale: in the key of C, the dominant is G.

Dramma giocoso - Literally meaning amusing, or lighthearted. Like tragicomedy it represents an opera whose story combines both serious and comic elements: Mozart's *Don Giovanni*.

Falsetto - Literally a lighter or "false" voice; an artificially produced high singing voice that extends above the range of the full voice.

Fioritura - Literally "flower"; a flowering ornamentation or embellishment of the vocal line within an aria.

Forte, Fortissimo - Forte (*f*) means loud: mezzo forte (*mf*) is fairly loud; fortissimo (*ff*) even louder, and additional *fff*'s indicate greater degrees of loudness.

Glissando - A rapid sliding up or down the scale.

Grand Opera - An opera in which there is no spoken dialogue and the entire text is set to music, frequently treating serious and dramatic subjects. Grand Opera flourished in France in the 19th century (Meyerbeer) and most notably by Verdi (Aida): the genre is epic in scale and combines spectacle, large choruses, scenery, and huge orchestras.

Heldentenor - A tenor with a powerful dramatic voice who possesses brilliant top notes and vocal stamina. Heldentenors are well suited to heroic (Wagnerian) roles: Lauritz Melchoir in Wagner's *Tristan und Isolde*.

Imbroglio - Literally "Intrigue"; an operatic scene with chaos and confusion and appropriate diverse melodies and rhythms.

Largo or larghetto - Largo indicates a very slow tempo; Larghetto is slightly faster than Largo.
Legato - Literally "tied"; therefore, successive tones that are connected smoothly. Opposing Legato would be Marcato (strongly accented and punctuated) and Staccato (short and aggressive).

Leitmotif - A short musical passage attached to a person, thing, feeling, or idea that provides associations when it recurs or is recalled.

Libretto - Literally "little book"; the text of an opera. On Broadway, the text of songs is called "lyrics" but the spoken text in the play is called the "book."

Lied - A German song; the plural is "lieder." Originally German art songs of the 19th century.

Light opera, or operetta - Operas that contain comic elements but light romantic plots: Johann Strauss's *Die Fledermaus.*

Maestro - From the Italian "master": a term of respect to conductors, composers, directors, and great musicians.

Melodrama - Words spoken over music. Melodrama appears in Beethoven's *Fidelio* but flourished during the late 19th century in the operas of Massenet (*Manon*). Melodrama should not be confused with melodrama when it describes a work that is characterized by extravagant theatricality and by the predominance of plot and physical action over characterization.

Mezza voce - Literally "medium voice," or singing with medium or half volume; it is generally intended as a vocal means to intensify emotion.

Mezzo-soprano - A woman's voice with a range between that of the soprano and contralto.

Molto - Very. Molto agitato means very agitated.

Obbligato - An elaborate accompaniment to a solo or principal melody that is usually played by a single instrument.

Octave - A musical interval embracing eight diatonic degrees: therefore, from C to C is an octave.

Opera - Literally "a work"; a dramatic or comic play combining music.

Opera buffa - Italian comic opera that flourished during the bel canto era. Buffo characters were usually basses singing patter songs: Dr. Bartolo in Rossini's *The Barber of Seville,* and Dr. Dulcamara in Donizetti's *The Elixir of Love.*

Opéra comique - A French opera characterized by spoken dialogue interspersed between the arias and ensemble numbers, as opposed to Grand Opera in which there is no spoken dialogue.

Operetta, or light opera - Operas that contain comic elements but tend to be more romantic: Strauss's *Die Fledermaus,* Offenbach's *La Périchole,* and Lehar's *The Merry Widow.* In operettas, there is usually much spoken dialogue, dancing, practical jokes, and mistaken identities.

Oratorio - A lengthy choral work, usually of a religious or philosophical nature and consisting chiefly of recitatives, arias, and choruses but in deference to its content, performed without action or scenery: Handel's *Messiah.*

Ornamentation - Extra embellishing notes—appoggiaturas, trills, roulades, or cadenzas—that enhance a melodic line.

Overture - The orchestral introduction to a musical dramatic work that frequently incorporates musical themes within the work.

Parlando - Literally "speaking"; the imitation of speech while singing, or singing that is almost speaking over the music. It is usually short and with minimal orchestral accompaniment.

Patter - Words rapidly and quickly delivered. Figaro's Largo in Rossini's *The Barber of Seville* is a patter song.

Pentatonic - A five-note scale, like the black notes within an octave on the piano.

Piano - Soft volume.

Pitch - The property of a musical tone that is determined by the frequency of the waves producing it.

Pizzicato - A passage played by plucking the strings instead of stroking the string with the bow.

Polyphony - Literally "many voices." A style of musical composition in which two or more independent melodies are juxtaposed in harmony; counterpoint.

Polytonal - The use of several tonal schemes simultaneously.

Portamento - A continuous gliding movement from one tone to another.

Prelude - An orchestral introduction to an act or the whole opera. An Overture can appear only at the beginning of an opera.

Presto, Prestissimo - Very fast and vigorous.

Prima Donna - The female star of an opera cast. Although the term was initially used to differentiate between the dramatic and vocal importance of a singer, today it generally describes the personality of a singer rather than her importance in the particular opera.

Prologue - A piece sung before the curtain goes up on the opera proper: Tonio's Prologue in Leoncavallo's *I Pagliacci*.

Quaver - An eighth note.

Range - The divisions of the voice: soprano, mezzo-soprano, contralto, tenor, baritone, and bass.

Recitative - A formal device that that advances the plot. It is usually a rhythmically free vocal style that imitates the natural inflections of speech; it represents the dialogue and narrative in operas and oratorios. Secco recitative is accompanied by harpsichord and sometimes with cello or continuo instruments and *accompagnato* indicates that the recitative is accompanied by the orchestra.

Ritornello - A short recurrent instrumental passage between elements of a vocal composition.

Romanza - A solo song that is usually sentimental; it is usually shorter and less complex than an aria and rarely deals with terror, rage, and anger.

Romantic Period - The period generally beginning with the raiding of the Bastille (1789) and the last revolutions and uprisings in Europe (1848). Romanticists generally found inspiration in nature and man. Beethoven's *Fidelio* (1805) is considered the first Romantic opera, followed by the works of Verdi and Wagner.

Roulade - A florid vocal embellishment sung to one syllable.

Rubato - Literally "robbed"; it is a fluctuation of tempo within a musical phrase, often against a rhythmically steady accompaniment.

Secco - The accompaniment for recitative played by the harpsichord and sometimes continuo instruments.

Semitone - A half-step, the smallest distance between two notes. In the key of C, the notes are E and F, and B and C.

Serial music - Music based on a series of tones in a chosen pattern without regard for traditional tonality.

Sforzando - Sudden loudness and force; it must stick out from the texture and provide a shock.

Singspiel - Early German musical drama employing spoken dialogue between songs: Mozart's *The Magic Flute.*

Soprano - The highest range of the female voice ranging from lyric (light and graceful quality) to dramatic (fuller and heavier in tone).

Sotto voce - Literally "below the voice"; sung softly between a whisper and a quiet conversational tone.

Soubrette - A soprano who sings supporting roles in comic opera: Adele in Strauss's *Die Fledermaus*, or Despina in Mozart's *Così fan tutte.*

Spinto - From the Italian "spingere" (to push); a soprano having lyric vocal qualities who "pushes" the voice to achieve heavier dramatic qualities.

Sprechstimme - Literally "speak voice." The singer half sings a note and half speaks; the declamation sounds like speaking but the duration of pitch makes it seem almost like singing.

Staccato - Short, clipped, rapid articulation; the opposite of the caressing effects of legato

Stretto - A concluding passage performed in a quicker tempo to create a musical climax.

Strophe - Music repeated for each verse of an aria.

Syncopation - Shifting the beat forward or back from its usual place in the bar; it is a temporary displacement of the regular metrical accent in music caused typically by stressing the weak beat.

Supernumerary - A "super"; a performer with a non-singing role: "Spear-carrier."

Tempo - Time, or speed. The ranges are Largo for very slow to Presto for very fast.

Tenor - Highest natural male voice.

Tessitura - The general range of a melody or voice part; but specifically, the part of the register in which most of the tones of a melody or voice part lie.

Tonality - The organization of all the tones and harmonies of a piece of music in relation to a tonic (the first tone of its scale).

Tone Poem - An orchestral piece with a program; a tscript.

Tonic - The keynote of the key in which a piece is written. C is the tonic of C major.

Trill - Two adjacent notes rapidly and repeatedly alternated.

Tutti - All together.

Twelve tone - The 12 chromatic tones of the octave placed in a chosen fixed order and constituting with some permitted permutations and derivations the melodic and harmonic material of a serial musical piece. Each note of the chromatic scale is used as part of the melody before any other note gets repeated.

Verismo - Literally "truth"; the artistic use of contemporary everyday material in preference to the heroic or legendary in opera. A movement from the late 19th century: *Carmen.*

Vibrato - A "vibration"; a slightly tremulous effect imparted to vocal or instrumental tone for added warmth and expressiveness by slight and rapid variations in pitch.